MYSTERIES
OF
TIME

Other books by Larry Verstraete

The Serendipity Effect

MYSTERIES OF TIME

LARRY VERSTRAETE

•

illustrated by
Ljuba Levstek

Scholastic Canada Ltd.

Scholastic Canada Ltd.
123 Newkirk Road, Richmond Hill, Ontario, Canada L4C 3G5

Scholastic Inc.
730 Broadway, New York, NY 10003, USA

Ashton Scholastic Limited
Private Bag 1, Penrose, Auckland, New Zealand

Ashton Scholastic Pty Limited
PO Box 579, Gosford, NSW 2250, Australia

Scholastic Publications Ltd.
Villiers House, Clarendon Avenue, Leamington Spa,
Warwickshire CV32 5PR, UK

Canadian Cataloguing in Publication Data

Verstraete, Larry
    Mysteries of time

ISBN 0-590-73093-2

1. Science – Methodology – Juvenile literature
2. Earth – Juvenile literature. I. Title.

Q175.2.V37 1992   j500   C92-094371-3

6 5 4 3 2 1   Printed in Canada   2 3 4 5 6 7
                      Manufactured by Webcom Limited

For my parents, George and Paula — my link to the past

For my children, Steven and Ashley — my bridge to the future

For my wife, Jo — my friend and companion in time

TABLE
OF
CONTENTS

Part 1.
PASSING
THROUGH
TIME

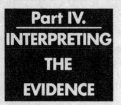

ACKNOWLEDGEMENTS

There is a saying: I couldn't have done it alone.
This is especially true of this book. Many people have helped to
make it possible, some directly, others indirectly.

Thank you . . .

To the archeologists, technicians and other specialists on site and
in the lab who so willingly answered my questions.

To the Forks Public Archaeological Association for providing me
with dig experience through the Public Archaeology Program at the
Forks National Historic Site.

To Vera Brandzin and Bruce Low for their special interest in this
undertaking and for their recommendations along the way.

To my editor, Pat Khashmanian, who pointed out inconsistencies,
pressed for accuracy and detail, and suggested changes that
strengthened and shaped the book.

To Diane Kerner, Senior Editor at Scholastic Canada, for
overseeing the project and for keeping the faith throughout.

To my colleagues in the teaching profession for the support and
ideas they generously offered.

To the students of the Fort Garry School Division in Winnipeg,
Manitoba who tested many of the activities in the book.

And lastly, but most importantly, to my family for their
encouragement, and above all, patience.

Thank you.

INTRODUCTION

What do you know about your past? About your first years of life? Your early years at school? About the people you knew and liked?

Possibly you remember some events very clearly. But you can't remember everything, not every moment of your life. Pieces of your past have become lost in time.

How would you find out about your missing past? You might ask your parents, relatives and friends. They probably remember some things you don't. You might check a photo album — pictures are great reminders of the past. Maybe you have other reminders of the past you can look at too. A favourite toy. Drawings you made. Books you read. Stories you wrote. Each of these clues can tell you something about yourself.

Slowly, you gather enough information to fill in the missing pieces. You begin to understand more about yourself, the way you were, and the reasons why you are what you are today. As you do this, you are a detective of time. You gather clues, analyze them, and piece them together one by one until you have a complete picture of the past.

In order to unravel stories from the past, archeologists work much the same way. They search for clues, for remains, for evidence that helps them understand events that have been lost in time. Then by analyzing and interpreting this information, these detectives of time piece together stories of people, animals and places from the past.

Archeologists learn from artifacts. Artifacts are objects that were made and used by people. Tools, weapons, clothing, pots, beads, books and other artifacts can tell a lot about how early people and their communities lived and died.

Archeologists learn from other remains, too. Buildings, tombs and other structures are clues to the past. So are rocks, bones and bodies. Even tiny hairs, seeds and cells can tell tales of long ago.

Archeologists do not work alone. They rely on technicians, artists, photographers and other experts to help them gather and interpret evidence. They also work closely with other scientists who are interested in understanding the past – geologists, paleontologists, biologists and zoologists.

This book is about archeologists and their work. Through its stories, activities, and notes you will learn about mysteries from the past, and find out how detectives of time search for evidence, study and analyze clues, and unravel the events of history.

HOW THE BOOK IS ORGANIZED

This book is divided into four main sections. Within the sections are chapters, each highlighting one facet of the archeologist's work. Each of the fourteen chapters has a Detective Case, a Detective File and a Time Probe, all dealing with the topic of that chapter.

The Detective Case:

The detective case tells of a mystery from the past that has been solved by archeologists and their colleagues. The case introduces the theme of the chapter and illustrates the methods of detection that were used to untangle the mystery.

The Detective File:

The detective file contains two parts: Notes and Detective Challenge. The Notes discuss techniques used by archeologists. Some of them may have been used to solve the introductory case, while others are more appropriate to other mysteries of time. The Detective Challenge poses questions and investigations for your consideration. Through activities you can learn more about the methods of the archeologist and improve your own detective skills.

Time Probe:

Those are other mysteries and riddles of the past. Some are in the process of being solved, while others baffle today's scientists and await solution by future detectives of time.

Part I

·························

PASSING
THROUGH
TIME

1. THE PAST PRESERVED

The Case of THE VANISHED PEOPLE

December 18, 1888 was a cold and blustery day in southwestern Colorado. Two cowboys, Richard Wetherill and his brother-in-law Charlie Mason, rode along a canyon rim in a region called Mesa Verde searching for stray cattle. The swirling snow whipped their faces. The men squinted across the canyon, searching for signs of movement among the rocks.

Suddenly the ghostly shape of a building appeared through the haze. It lingered for a moment, then disappeared. Minutes later the shadowy form reappeared and vanished again.

The two men shook their heads in disbelief. Had they really seen something? Curious now, Wetherill and Mason rode down into the canyon to take a closer look. There, deep in the gorge, tucked underneath a huge overhang of rock, the cowboys found hundreds of interlocking buildings. They had stumbled upon a long-abandoned city.

Much of the city lay in ruins, with stones and timber toppled over one another. Here and there, however, the men found pottery, stone axes, bows and arrows, handwoven baskets, even human skeletons. According to Wetherill it looked "as though the inhabitants had left everything they possessed right where they had used it last."

Wetherill and Mason named their find Cliff Palace. Over the next few weeks they camped there to explore the canyon further. And they found other cliff dwellings. Some, like Cliff Palace, were crammed into deep caves. Others were built into shallow hollows in the canyon wall. Still others were perched high above the canyon floor along narrow ledges of rock that could only be reached after a dangerous and difficult climb.

News of the discovery soon spread. Treasure hunters arrived looking for objects to hoard or sell. By the time archeologists entered the area in 1891, many of the dwellings had already been looted. Valuable artifacts had been lost and some of the dwellings had been badly damaged. To help preserve the sites the area was declared a national monument, called Mesa Verde National Park, in 1906.

Since then, hundreds of separate clusters of dwellings have been found in Mesa Verde. It appears that at one time, long ago, an industrious people lived in the area. They left no written records, and today only bits of their buildings remain. But from excavation of their dwellings, broken pieces of pottery and other artifacts, archeologists have been able to tell much about these early inhabitants.

Cliff Palace, Mesa Verde

Mesa Verde National Park. Negative number 2422.

Around A.D. 500 the Mesa Verde area was home to a tribe of people that later Indians called the Anasazi or "Ancient Ones." The early Anasazi were peaceful farmers and hunters who lived in mud buildings on the flat plateau above the deep canyons. But around A.D. 1200 their lifestyle suddenly changed. The Anasazi left the unprotected plateau and sought refuge in the more remote canyons below, perhaps because of new, unfriendly people arriving in the area.

In the canyons the Anasazi gathered fallen sandstone rocks, chipped and shaped them with harder riverbed stones, then cemented them into place in caves and niches in the canyon walls. The dwellings grew room by room, linked to one another by doorways, balconies and ladders. Gradually cities took shape. Some of them were small, only two or three rooms. Others, like Cliff Palace, were much larger and contained hundreds of interlocking, multi-storied buildings set well back into deep caves.

Despite the differences in size, each cluster of dwellings was similar in shape and design. They could all be easily defended. Because they were built into the canyon wall, only the front of each site had to be defended in case of attack by enemies.

For almost one hundred years the Anasazi flourished in the canyons. But by A.D. 1300 they had almost all abandoned their dwellings and moved out of the area, leaving behind many of their possessions — grinding stones, baskets, pottery, anything that couldn't be easily carried.

The disappearance of these people is puzzling. Why did the Anasazi desert their homes and belongings so unexpectedly and so completely? What unknown force drove them away?

Charlie Mason, one of the cowboys who discovered Cliff Palace, thought that the Anasazi were wiped out by "more savage and warlike neighbours, the men being killed and the women being adopted into the tribes of the conquerors."

But archeologists now think that the enemy may not have come from outside as Charlie Mason believed. Evidence unearthed at Mesa Verde in the years since Cliff Palace was discovered suggests that the Anasazi may have been their own worst enemy.

Studies of the canyon dwellings and surrounding area show that when the Anasazi began to construct those homes, they cut down the surrounding trees for timber and firewood. First they used the trees closest to the buildings. Then as they needed more, they cut those farther along the canyon floors.

As the forested areas vanished, so did the animals that lived in them. The Anasazi were forced to travel greater distances to hunt game. Hunting expeditions took longer and hunters often returned home empty-handed. Without the protection of the trees, the soil began to erode easily. Valuable minerals in the earth were lost to the forces of wind and water, and crops did not grow as well.

Perhaps these conditions would not have been enough to force the Anasazi to move, but archeologists believe they faced another problem too. Studies of the tree rings from timber in the area show that the weather also changed. The Mesa Verde region suffered a severe drought from A.D. 1276 to 1299. Water supplies from nearby streams and springs probably dwindled to a trickle. In the same period the temperature cooled, making the growing season shorter and the harvest even poorer.

To the Anasazi these problems must have seemed overwhelming. The loss of timber, wildlife, crops and water proved to be too great a burden. Taking only what they could carry, they left their homes and belongings and walked south out of the canyons. In time these proud people mixed with other tribes and vanished as a separate group.

Today Mesa Verde National Park is open to the public. As the visitor gazes at the golden-red walls of dwellings and listens to the wind whistle through empty rooms, it is not difficult to picture the powerful nation of people who lived here seven hundred years ago. Mesa Verde stands as both a tribute to an ambitious people and a reminder of man's past mistakes.

DETECTIVE FILE #1
NOTES: Becoming Lost in Time

Building blocks, chunks of wood, tools and weapons, pieces of pottery and clothing, bones and bodies — these are clues from the past. This is the evidence that helps detectives of time understand the events of long ago.

But how does the past become lost in time? How does the evidence become buried or hidden? Knowing the answers to these questions can help us look for clues.

Nature has several ways of burying and preserving the past. Sometimes the forces of nature are sudden and destructive.

Volcanoes, earthquakes, tidal waves and other natural disasters can quickly change the appearance of the earth and the ways of people. So can famine, drought or sudden changes in climate. During such difficult times people may be forced to move from one place to another, leaving their dwellings and possessions behind.

The story of Pompeii and Herculaneum, ancient cities in Italy, is a good example. In A.D. 79 the volcano Vesuvius erupted. Ash and lava showered down on nearby Pompeii and Herculaneum, covering them and their inhabitants in a matter of hours. For centuries the two cities slept beneath their blanket of deposits. In time they were forgotten.

Then three hundred years ago, workers digging wells and canals rediscovered the cities. Many of the buildings remained intact. Some of the long-dead inhabitants were preserved. Everywhere artifacts hastily abandoned revealed life as it had been on the day the volcano erupted. The rediscovery of Pompeii and Herculaneum allowed us a rare glimpse of a moment that had been frozen in time.

But nature is not always so dramatic. Usually it works slowly over many years to hide places and things. Sediments in lakes and oceans cover objects. Winds sweep across the land, gradually covering structures with sand and soil. Land masses slowly rise and fall, causing coastal cities to become submerged and concealed beneath the water. In tropical areas where vegetation grows rapidly, abandoned temples and dwellings become hidden by vines and trees.

Humans too can change and disguise evidence of the past. Sometimes man rebuilds in the same spot, even using materials that were once part of something else. Settlements can rise one on top of another, hiding evidence of earlier days deep underground. War, on the other hand, often causes buildings to be destroyed and written records to be lost.

People discard and bury things constantly. Food scraps are thrown into garbage pits. Broken, worn or torn articles are tossed aside. In time these objects become buried under layers of waste and soil, unmarked and unseen. But if they are discovered, such objects can provide valuable information about the habits and lifestyles of people and their communities.

People are often collectors and hoarders, too. From the earliest of times, travellers and warriors have taken souvenirs back home. In this way articles from one culture become mixed with those of another. This can make the task of interpreting the past extremely complex and difficult.

DETECTIVE CHALLENGE: Surviving Time / An Experiment

Not all objects that are lost in time survive intact. Many decay or corrode. Others become discoloured, weathered or torn. What kind of materials survive the longest? What conditions are best for preserving objects? A simple experiment will help answer these questions.

Materials:
- a variety of small objects such as metal nails, bits of plastic, brick and stone, orange or banana peels, and pieces of cloth, paper and wood
- containers or boxes with lids
- cellophane wrap
- soil

What to Do:
1) Separate the materials into three sets, with each set containing roughly the same kinds of objects as the others. One of these sets will be buried in soil, another will be left open to the air, the third will be kept in the freezer.

2) Find a burial place for the objects that are going in the soil. This can be outdoors in some specially marked corner of the garden, or indoors in a box or aquarium that has been partly filled with soil. Carefully cover the objects with a good layer of soil. To help you find them later, you might place little sticks in the soil to mark their spots. Water the soil lightly and keep it moist over the next few weeks.

3) Place the objects that will be left exposed to the air in a container or box. Cover the container with plastic wrap so that odours and bacteria will not contaminate the room, then put on the lid.

4) The objects that are going into the freezer can be put into a well-sealed container or a plastic bag. Label the container to avoid confusion with foods in the freezer.

5) Now wait several weeks. Then carefully unearth each set of objects. How do they compare? Which materials seem to be well preserved? Which materials decayed? Which environment preserved objects the best? The worst?

TIME PROBE: Surviving Time

Where is the Colossus of Rhodes?

Although physical evidence from the past is often altered or destroyed by nature, ideas have a way of surviving through time. The story of the Colossus of Rhodes is a good example.

More than 2000 years ago a giant bronze statue of the Greek sun god Helios towered 37 metres above the harbour at Rhodes, a small island in the Mediterranean Sea. Standing on a huge marble pedestal, one hand clutching a sword, the other holding a torch, the warrior-like figure guided ships into the harbour.

Construction of the Colossus, as the statue was called, started in 286 B.C. Because of its size and weight the Colossus could not be built of solid metal. Instead a hollow bronze shell was used. Individual sections were cast on site, then bolted together and reinforced with iron struts inside the statue.

It took twelve years to complete the statue. For 50 more years the Colossus of Rhodes loomed over the harbour, a tribute to the ingenuity of its builders, a beacon to wayward ships.

Then in 224 B.C. an earthquake rocked the island. The Colossus toppled, snapping into house-sized pieces. For hundreds of years the broken statue lay where it had fallen, attracting visitors who came to stand and stare at this once-great wonder of the ancient world. In A.D. 653 the metal supports were dismantled. Bit by bit the Colossus was sold for scrap and shipped to neighbouring countries around the Mediterranean.

Although the original Colossus of Rhodes has long since disappeared, in a curious way it may still survive. The scrap metal was melted and recast into new tools, weapons and ornaments. It is possible that some of these objects may exist even today.

But the statue at Rhodes survives in a different way too. Another colossus, modelled after the ancient one, was erected in 1886, this time in New York harbour. Built of metal sheathing supported by iron struts, standing on a stone pedestal, one hand clutching a book, the other holding a torch, the Statue of Liberty welcomes visitors to America today. It reminds us that great ideas can be used over and over again.

2. THE PAST UNCOVERED

The Case of THE MONSTER AND THE MAZE

Greek legends going back more than 2500 years tell the tale of a mighty king and a fierce monster that once ruled the island of Crete in the Mediterranean Sea.

According to the story, King Minos kept a beast called the Minotaur in a great maze or labyrinth beneath his palace. The animal had the body of a man and the horned head of a bull. The Minotaur stalked the underground labyrinth, devouring any human prey that crossed its path.

To satisfy the monster's appetite, Minos demanded that the king of nearby Athens provide human victims for the Minotaur. Each year the seven handsomest young men and the seven most beautiful maidens of Athens were sent to Crete and released into the labyrinth. The maze was so large, so dark and so complicated that escape was impossible. One by one the 14 youths were discovered and devoured by the Minotaur.

For centuries the tale of the monster and the maze was told and retold. Like other legends of the past, people assumed it was a fanciful story, one that was interesting but not based on facts. Arthur Evans, a British scholar, amateur archeologist and traveller, was familiar with the story of the Minotaur. He too paid little attention to the tale. Then one day in the early 1890s something in an antique store in Athens aroused his interest.

Among the vases and furniture in the shop Evans spotted some tiny stones pierced with holes as if for a necklace. Unusual scratches covered the beads. The marks seemed to be a type of picture writing Evans could not decipher. He had seen similar markings on stones before, but had never been able to determine where they came from. This antique dealer, however, had a definite answer for him: "The island of Crete."

In 1894 Evans travelled to Crete for the first time. He noticed that many of the native women wore necklaces or bracelets fashioned from stones with similar curious markings. One bore the design of a labyrinth. Another had the shape of a creature that was half human and half bull. These recalled to his mind the story of the Minotaur and the labyrinth. Could there be a connection?

Evans was determined to begin an excavation on Crete. But where should he dig?

Earlier archeologists had made interesting discoveries at a hill known as Kephala. Ceramic jars, signs of buildings and smaller artifacts had been unearthed there. Interestingly, tradition gave the site the name of Knossos, the ancient capital of Crete. That was the obvious place to start an excavation.

By 1900 Evans had bought the hill of Kephala and was ready to begin. He had a crew of thirty workers and three professionals to help him. Almost immediately after the dig began, one of the workers struck something hard with a spade. Excitedly the men dug around the object. It proved to be a large block of stone. More blocks were soon found, each one piled on or next to the others. Slowly one wall, then another, was uncovered in the mound.

Evans and his crew unearthed rooms and corridors. Bit by bit a gigantic palace grew out of the dirt. After twenty-five years of excavation and restoration, the palace proved to cover more than ten city blocks. In some places it stood more than three storeys high. A large rectangular courtyard stood at its centre. A thousand rooms jutted and twisted around the courtyard, all linked by an array of staircases and passageways.

The palace was a technological and artistic wonder. Advanced systems of plumbing and lighting had been used in its construction. A system of pipes carried hot and cold water through the palace, and other enormous clay pipes transported wastes and sewage away. Immense openings from the roof down to other levels of the palace allowed sunlight to spread to faraway chambers. Walls were decorated with elegant paintings and sculptures. Beautifully decorated vases, statues and benches filled the rooms.

Was this the palace of the legendary King Minos? Evans soon

realized that the complex palace could not have been built within a single king's lifetime. Excavations showed that the palace had been started around 3400 B.C., and that for two thousand years new rooms, hallways and wings had been gradually added.

Minoan bullfighting

Evans proposed that, although there may have been an original King Minos, the word *Minos* itself was probably a general title meaning "ruler." Throughout the long history of Knossos there had been many rulers, each one called the Minos. Each Minos added new parts to the palace so that in time it became a complex, sprawling structure. The civilization that produced the palace Evans named "Minoan."

But what of the Minotaur tale? As Evans excavated the site, he found several reminders of the legend. The palace itself, with its twists and turns, its layers of rooms and corridors, its mysterious dead ends and winding passageways, resembled a confusing maze.

Within the palace the symbol of a double axe was common on walls, pillars and many smaller artifacts. In the language of the ancient people of the island, the word for double axe was *labrys*. When a suffix meaning "place of" was added, the word became *labryinth*. Labyrinth, or "the place of the double axe," was the Minoan description for the confusing palace.

Symbols of bulls were also found on vases, jars and walls throughout the palace. Ornamental bull horns supported stone altars. Rings, royal seals and coins carried bull images. Evans was so struck by the many paintings and carvings of bulls in the palace that he once exclaimed, "What a part these creatures play here!"

One of the greatest discoveries was a section of wall decorated with a fresco, a painting done on wet plaster. The fresco shows a bull in full charge, with a youth in the air over its head. Two other young people stand nearby. The scene suggests that the Minoans might have engaged in some dangerous ritual or sport involving bulls.

Although the events of long ago are shadowed in mystery, this fresco suggests a possible basis for the Minotaur legend. With a little imagination we can go back in time to reconstruct such an event and trace the origin of the famous tale.

● ● ●

For weeks 15-year-old Daelias had prepared for her encounter with the beast. Along with other chosen youths she had exercised, practised leaps and tumbles, and perfected her routine. Now she was ready. Today she would challenge the beast. Today she would have a chance to demonstrate her skill and daring — an honour bestowed on only a few each year.

In a room deep within the winding hallways of the palace Daelias waited with the others. While some paced nervously or warmed up with bending and stretching exercises, Daelias chose to sit quietly and think. She knew that a clear mind, one ready to make split-second decisions, would be an advantage.

Suddenly the door to the room flew open. A priest dressed in ceremonial robes and wearing a mask of the beast beckoned the athletes to follow. Down one corridor after another the young people walked in silence.

Despite her efforts to keep calm, Daelias grew more tense. Along the palace walls she could make out carvings and pictures of the beast, a reminder of the task ahead. She could hear the roar of the spectators in the arena growing louder with each step. Ahead she could see the priest, the horns of his mask swaying high above the others.

At last they stopped. The priest flung open a door. The corridor flooded with sunlight and the noise of the crowd. As she walked into the arena Daelias felt proud. She was one of a chosen few. Today was her day.

In the depths of the labyrinth the athletes had drawn lots. Daelias and two others would go first. Daelias positioned herself in the centre of the arena. Her two companions, a girl and a young man, stood on either side.

A hushed silence waved over the crowd. Across the arena a door opened. A massive head appeared in the doorway, its horns stretching more than a metre across. The beast!

The bull stood still for a moment as if planning its strategy. Then it pawed the ground, snorted and charged, its target the young woman in the centre of the ring. With pounding hoofs the animal thundered closer and closer.

Daelias waited, her breath suspended, her body motionless, her eyes fixed on the rampaging beast. Just as the animal seemed ready to slice into her she sprang forward. In a single, swift move Daelias grabbed the bull's horns and did the impossible. She tossed herself in a somersault, flipped through the air over the animal's back, and landed in the arms of one of her companions.

For a second there was silence. Then the crowd rose to its feet and roared its approval. Daelias bowed deeply and smiled. She had emerged victorious. Today she had met the mighty beast and conquered it.

●●●

No one can be certain of the details of this event. But it is quite possible that the Minotaur legend began as a retelling of such encounters between Minoan youths and bulls. Perhaps over time the story changed. The bull became more fierce, a monster that was half man and half beast. The confusing palace became a true labyrinth. The youths became victims, sacrifices to the beast that lurked there.

For hundreds of years the Minoan civilization flourished. Then it mysteriously disappeared. Archeologists believe that a massive volcanic eruption on a nearby island may have been responsible. Tonnes of ash and poisonous gas spewed over Crete, and gigantic tidal waves crashed upon its shores. The advanced civilization that had thrived there was completely devastated.

The palace at Knossos vanished. The tangle of rooms and passageways with their treasures and memories faded into the past. Only the strange tale of a monster and a maze kept the image of the Minoans alive, until the curiosity of a nineteenth-century archeologist brought it to light again.

DETECTIVE FILE #2

NOTES: Adding Up The Clues

How do archeologists come to conclusions about the past?

An archeologist arrives at conclusions in much the same way as a crime detective. To see how they both work, imagine yourself in this situation.

You are digging a garden for a neighbour. Just below the surface of the soil you find a small plastic bag. In the bag is a diamond ring.

How strange, you think. Questions roll around in your mind. How did the bag get here? Did someone drop it, or was it intentionally buried? Why is the ring in a bag?

Perhaps the ring was stolen, you decide. The thief probably hid it in the garden until he could come back for it. That sounds like a good guess. Maybe you should report your find to the police.

But then you take a closer look. The initials C.L. are engraved on the inside of the ring. The ring itself is scratched, and one of the diamonds seems to be missing.

Wait a minute! Why would a thief steal a damaged ring? And why put it in a bag? You quickly decide that your first explanation was wrong.

So how did the ring get into the garden?

Maybe it was being taken in for repairs when it was accidentally dropped. You did find it near the surface, and it might have been in the bag for safekeeping. Yes, that explanation fits the facts.

But what about the initials C.L.? Hmm. Your neighbour's name is Clara Lumis, and this is her garden. The ring probably belongs to her, you realize. She'll be glad to know you found it.

To arrive at this conclusion you followed clues and made an

initial guess, a hypothesis. As more clues surfaced you compared your guess with the new evidence and altered it to fit the facts. Eventually you came up with the best possible scenario to explain the lost ring. You were able to make an inference, a well-established explanation based upon all the available evidence.

Archeologists work the same way. From whatever evidence they have they make a beginning guess or hypothesis about the past. A hypothesis gives the scientist a focus, a direction to follow in his or her research. When new clues are unearthed they can be compared to the hypothesis. Perhaps they will support it, making the hypothesis stronger and more possible. Or perhaps they will show that the hypothesis is wrong. In that case another hypothesis based on all the known facts will have to be made.

Either way, right or wrong, the time detective comes a little closer to unravelling the truth about the past by testing a hypothesis. Eventually, when enough evidence supports a hypothesis, it can strengthen into a convincing inference.

DETECTIVE CHALLENGE: Developing Hypotheses and Inferences

How accurate are your hypotheses? Try this activity to find out.

Materials:
- a box or bag containing objects belonging to another person
- a notepad and pencil

What to Do:
1) Ask a friend, parent or relative to help with this activity. Tell your helper that you are practising your detective skills. You would like to examine artifacts that belong to another person, but you want the identity of that person to be kept secret until the end of your investigation.

Ask your helper to select a subject, preferably a person you don't know very well. With the permission of that person, your helper is to gather five or more "artifacts." These should be everyday objects that are used by the subject, objects such as pieces of clothing, books, ornaments, toys, tools, utensils, favourite packaged foods, etc. Ask your helper to put the artifacts in a bag or box, but not to reveal the identity of the owner.

2) Now practise being a detective. Take the first artifact out of the box. On your notepad name the object, then make some hypotheses about the owner.

> For example, if the object is a curling iron you might write:
> *Artifact: curling iron*
> *Hypotheses: female, perhaps a teenager or older, possibly with long hair rather than shorter*

3) Do the same with each artifact, remembering to adjust your early hypotheses so they agree with new evidence.

4) After you have analyzed all the artifacts, study the clues together. How much do you know about the owner? Can you identify who it might be? Write an inference based on your hypotheses.

5) Report your results to your helper and find out the true answer. How accurate were your hypotheses? How correct was your inference?

TIME PROBE: Conflicting Conclusions
In Search of the Real Crete

When a crime is committed police detectives track clues, study the evidence, and eventually arrive at conclusions. Usually this leads to the arrest of a suspect, who is charged with the crime.

When the case reaches court a jury examines the evidence. The jury may decide that the evidence matches the conclusion and the suspect is guilty as charged. Or the jury may find that the evidence does not support the charges, that the conclusion does not match the evidence presented in court. Then the charges are dropped and the suspect is released.

Archeologists work the same way. They examine evidence, form conclusions and interpret the past. But just as a jury may not always agree with the conclusions of a police detective, time detectives — scientists — do not always agree with one another. Sometimes they interpret the past in very different ways.

Take ancient Minoan society as one example. After his excavations at Knossos Arthur Evans thought he had a good understanding of the Minoan people. He believed that the Minoans thrived on competition and combat. Men held the positions of power in Minoan society. A king, the Minos, governed the people and used his authority to maintain order. According to Evans the double-edged axes carved on the palace walls symbolized the power of the Minos.

Recently some scholars have questioned such interpretations of the past. Marija Gimbutas, a professor at the University of California, believes that archeologists like Evans may have been influenced by their own cultures. She argues that because these earlier archeologists were men who lived in societies that were governed mostly by other men, societies that stressed competition and the use of power, they unwittingly assumed that earlier civilizations must have been the same. Instead of being open to new possibilities, their vision was clouded by their own experiences.

After examining the evidence of images and symbols found on artifacts from Crete and many other sites around the world, Gimbutas has concluded that life in ancient times was not as Evans imagined. She believes that early European societies — including the Minoan — were operated cooperatively by both women and men. The emphasis was not on competition and combat, but on peace and harmony between people and nature. The double-edged axe, Gimbutas says, was not a symbol of power, but rather a symbol of the constantly renewed cycle of life and death.

Gimbutas disagrees with Evans' interpretation of the past. Other scholars, however, disagree with Gimbutas or are not completely convinced by her evidence. Who is correct?

For now, until further evidence can be studied, both views must be considered possible. The case is still open. The search for the real Crete continues.

Part II

·····································

SEARCHING
FOR
EVIDENCE

3. FINDING A SITE

The Case of THE SACRED WELL

Edward Herbert Thompson never met Diego de Landa. The two men lived three centuries apart. Yet in a strange way their paths crossed in a steamy jungle in Yucatan, a peninsula in the southern part of Mexico.

Edward Thompson was born in the United States in 1860. Even as a lad he was interested in tales of early Indian tribes, especially stories of the Maya, an ancient people who had lived in Mexico and Central America. He read every book he could find on them and soon became an expert. One book in particular stirred Thompson's imagination. It was a book written three hundred years earlier by a Spanish bishop of Yucatan — Diego de Landa.

When the Spanish invaded Yucatan in 1546 they found descendants of the ancient Maya living in the area. Although the power of the Mayan civilization had faded, these people still carried on many of the traditions and beliefs of their ancestors. As the newly appointed bishop of Yucatan, Diego de Landa hoped to convert the natives to Christianity. He ordered the Mayan temples looted, their treasures destroyed, and their sacred writings burned.

But later when de Landa met with the conquered people, he listened with attention to stories about their ancestors. He became interested in their traditions and wrote down the details of each story in a book.

For years after his death de Landa's book lay forgotten in a dusty corner in the Royal Library in Madrid, Spain. Then in 1863 the book was rediscovered and published.

Many scholars thought that de Landa had merely made up the stories. They dismissed them as fiction. But not Edward Thompson. Intrigued by the tales, he read each one over and over. One story in particular fascinated him. It was the story of Yum Chac, the Mayan rain god.

The Maya believed that Yum Chac controlled the harvest and the welfare of the people. When Yum Chac was content the rains came and the corn grew. When Yum Chac was displeased the rains stopped and the people starved.

The natives believed that Yum Chac lived at the bottom of a deep, water-filled pit. To win the god's favour they honoured him in a mysterious ceremony. The ceremony started at a temple on a hill in the city of Chichen Itza. From there a procession wound down "a wide and handsome roadway" to the Sacred Well, where offerings were made to Yum Chac. The offerings

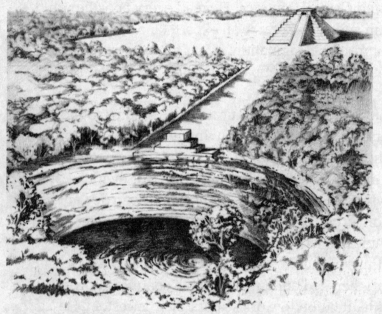

How the Sacred Well might have looked in Mayan times

included gold, precious stones and other valuable things, but they also included human sacrifices, especially in times of drought.

To Thompson this story was so real that when he closed his eyes he could imagine each detail of the ceremony. He saw the wave of brightly costumed men slowly walking down the sacred path. He smelled the incense that burned as an offering at the edge of the well. He heard the high priests chant their prayers to Yum Chac. He pictured the Maya as they stepped forward to the rim of the Sacred Well and threw in their precious offerings of gold, jade and copper. He saw the crowd part as the final offering, a human gift to Yum Chac, was lifted high, then hurled into the black waters below. He felt the tension in the crowd break as the body sank below the surface and Yum Chac accepted the gift.

Thompson believed de Landa's story and dreamed of the day when he might explore the Sacred Well and discover the treasure and secrets it held. In 1894 he got his chance.

Supported by Harvard University and the American Antiquarian Society, Thompson set out on a scientific expedition to the Mayan ruins. He travelled to Merida, the capital of Yucatan, hired a guide, and set out on horseback to the site of Chichen Itza.

The journey was painfully slow. The tropical forest was dense and a path had to be carved through it. Camped at last near the ancient city, Thompson was restless. He paced nervously about the camp.

A brilliant moon hung in the sky, casting an eerie glow over the countryside. Suddenly Thompson caught a flash of light out of the corner of his eye. He stopped and looked more closely. In the distance he could make out a glimmer, the reflection of moonlight off some surface perhaps. Quickly he saddled up his horse and rode to the beckoning light.

In a few minutes Thompson came upon a staggering sight. A huge pyramid-shaped temple rose out of the forest. Thompson dismounted and slowly climbed the decaying steps to the top. Around him he saw a dozen more large structures, and ahead lay a straight path that seemed to disappear into blackness. Was this the Sacred Way that de Landa had written about?

Thompson was too exhausted to continue further. He rode back to his camp and dropped into a deep sleep. But at dawn he roused his guide and headed back to the cluster of pyramids.

The sight was even more staggering by the light of day. The path that Thompson had seen the night before proved to be overgrown with shrubs and weeds, but he could see that it had once been much wider. It ended at a small building. Then suddenly Thompson found himself standing on a platform staring down into an oval-shaped well.

The well matched de Landa's description. It was 76 metres across at its widest point. Steep rock walls rose 18 metres above it. From the platform high above the jade green waters Thompson knew he was gazing into history. His view was the same as that of countless victims of centuries past. What secrets must lie beneath those still waters!

Thompson decided to scoop out the bottom of the well. He went back to the United States to purchase dredging equipment and to be trained as a diver. Some weeks later he returned to Chichen Itza.

The well was wide and 25 metres deep. To scoop out the whole bottom would be an impossible task, so Thompson conducted an experiment to narrow down the possibilities. He cut logs that were the size and weight of an average person and hurled them from the platform into the well. By mapping where the logs landed, he was able to identify the most likely area to dredge.

Thompson set up the dredging equipment and began the task of scooping out the bottom. Five men were hired to operate the cables and winches that manoeuvered the huge shovel into place, lowered it into the water, and closed its jaws on the debris at the bottom. Each load of sediment was dumped on the bank and examined closely. For weeks the shovel brought up scoop after scoop of mud, rotten leaves, broken branches and chunks of rock. There was no evidence of any offerings. Thompson became discouraged. Perhaps he had misjudged the spot. Or maybe de Landa's story was fictional after all.

One morning Thompson sat idly watching his men at work. The shovel drew up another load of muck and dumped it on the evergrowing pile. Thompson wandered over and noticed two yellowish-white lumps poking through the mud. Picking them up, he turned them over in his hand. Then he cautiously tasted one. They were balls of *pom*, the sacred incense used by the Maya in their ceremonies! With a cry of excitement Thompson held them high in the air for all the workers to see.

From that day on the dredge brought up many other Mayan

objects — bowls, vases, arrowheads, axes, beads, jade earrings, bells, and gold figurines and disks. It also brought up skeletons of men, women and children — the tragic human gifts to Yum Chac.

Finally the dredge brought up only bits of the rock bottom. Thompson knew that he had gone as far as he could with dredging equipment. To explore the bottom further he would have to go underwater himself. He and an assistant donned clumsy waterproof canvas suits. A 13-kilogram copper helmet was screwed to the top of each. Long hoses led from the helmets to an air pump. Heavy lead necklaces and thick iron shoes were fitted to the suits for extra weight.

Thompson was the first to enter the water. The experience was exciting and dangerous. As he later described it, "I felt a strange thrill when I realized I was the only living being who had ever reached this place alive and expected to leave it again still living."

The two divers sank slowly to the bottom. They discovered that if they sat down and touched their face plates together they could talk to each other. But the water was so murky that they could see nothing. All they could do was grope and feel their way around, hoping by chance to find something important.

The men were lucky. Their dives located many Mayan objects, including sacrificial knives, golden ceremonial masks, and figures of Mayan gods. One day Thompson found the outstretched skeletons of three women in a hollow at the bottom. One of the women wore a jade necklace, and parts of her dress were still intact. Thompson was able to collect the cloth fragments, the first pieces of Mayan clothing ever found.

Thompson wondered why the Maya had singled out this particular well as the home of Yum Chac. There were other wells in Chichen Itza. Why not one of them? The answer to this puzzle came quite by accident.

One day as he was sitting on a pontoon floating on the water Thompson heard murmuring voices. They seemed to be coming from somewhere in the well. He looked down into the water and was shocked to see the heads of several Mayan Indians deep below the surface. The heads bobbed slowly, nodding from side to side. Their lips moved as if they were speaking, producing a low babble that he could hear. He sat upright in shock, then looked into the water again. The heads were still there.

Thompson glanced up towards the top of the steep rock walls and saw his workers peering down over the edge at the pontoon. Suddenly he realized what had happened. The heads in the water were reflections of his own workers. Because of the steep overhanging walls, the sound of their voices echoed off the water in a soft murmur that seemed to come from below. To the ancient Maya it must have seemed that Yum Chac himself was speaking from the watery depths. No other well in Chichen Itza produced this unusual effect.

Although Thompson's early explorations revealed many valuable Mayan artifacts, a 1960 Mexican expedition found even more. Using an air lift — a type of underwater vacuum cleaner — divers were able to suck up much more debris from the bottom. Over four thousand artifacts were located in this way.

Seven years later another expedition lowered the water level in the well using pumps. Six thousand more artifacts were recovered. These included the first pieces of Mayan furniture ever found, the gold-foil soles of a child's shoes, and the remains of four to five hundred sacrificial victims. Many of these artifacts are now on view in the National Archeological Museum of Mexico City.

Thompson's faith in de Landa's writings opened the door to our understanding of ancient Mayan ways. Today the Chichen Itza site is open to the public. Modern visitors can stand on the edge of the Sacred Well of Sacrifice and gaze into the silent waters below, sharing the same chills of awe and excitement felt by Thompson himself almost a century ago.

DETECTIVE FILE #3

NOTES: Locating Sites

How do archeologists know where to dig?

Historical references are one source of clues. Maps, books, government and church registers, sketches and old newspapers help pinpoint the sites of buildings, forts, cities, battlefields and graveyards.

Stories and legends passed from one generation to the next can also be useful. Because these tales have been told many times by different people, not all of their details may be true or accurate, but to archeologists they can be helpful leads and the start of more thorough research.

Archeologists also learn a lot about a site by asking questions of themselves. Would ancient people want to live here? Does the site satisfy human needs? Is there a source of water nearby? Is the site easily defended? Is the soil suitable for farming? If the answer to many of these questions is yes, then it is possible that early people may once have lived there.

But often more exact methods are necessary to pinpoint the location of likely sites. Some clues can be found on the ground itself. Erosion, land movements and human construction have a way of stirring up the soil, bringing evidence to the surface. Bits of bone, fragments of stone, or artifacts found on top of the ground could indicate that something important is underneath.

Unexpected changes in the landscape can be helpful signs too. Hollows or depressions in the ground could mean that the soil has settled over a structure or pit. Mounds or hills could indicate that walls, buildings or garbage dumps are below.

Aerial photographs — photos taken from a plane — can point out things that an archeologist on foot might otherwise miss. When sunlight strikes the ground at just the right angle, hollows or ridges on the surface show up as lines of shadow in aerial photographs. Shadows such as these may indicate that walls or buildings lie buried underground.

Aerial photographs can show changes in plant growth too. Plants in one area might be thicker, taller or greener than plants in another area. Such changes in growth could be due to hidden structures underground. For example, plants growing above a buried wall will be shorter than neighbouring plants because they are growing in shallower soil.

The archeologist also uses tools to probe deeper into the soil in an effort to identify likely spots to dig. Solid metal rods forced into the ground stop when an object is struck. By probing in many spots in this way, the archeologist can pinpoint the size, shape and depth of buried objects. If hollow metal rods are used, samples of soil can be drawn up with them. These samples may contain chunks of wood, coal, charcoal or artifacts, all evidence of man's presence long ago.

Sometimes specialized equipment is used. Metal detectors sweep the ground and pick up traces of hidden coins, pipes and nails. Sounding equipment sends ultrasonic sound waves into the soil. As the waves bounce off underground objects they reflect up to the surface and tell the archeologist that something lies below. A similar technique involving electricity is also used. Electrical currents are directed into the soil and measured at various spots. Objects in the soil change these electrical measurements, providing valuable information for the archeologist.

Usually an archeological site cannot be identified by using just one of these methods. But when several are used together, these techniques can provide the archeologist with many clues. In the hands of a skilled detective of time the clues have a way of coming together. Like pieces of a puzzle, when enough of them fit, everything seems to fall into place.

DETECTIVE CHALLENGE: Tracking a Story

Stories and traditions are valuable to the detective of time. They hold clues to events of the past and may help to locate lost sites or to interpret evidence that has been found.

Stories and traditions help in another way too. They provide a means of checking hypotheses and conclusions. The study of Millie's Camp shows how this works.

In the 1970s a Canadian archeologist, Robson Bonnichsen, studied a recently abandoned Indian camp. He examined the artifacts, dwellings and environment around the camp. From this evidence he drew conclusions about the people that lived there.

Later Bonnichsen met with one of the original inhabitants of the camp, an Indian woman named Millie. He interviewed her and listened to her stories about life at the site. When he compared his conclusions with Millie's description, he found that some of his interpretations were correct, but many were wrong. Bonnichsen's study shows that when evidence at a site is supported by records about the past, the chance for accuracy is greater.

Try your hand at collecting a story from the past. Arrange an interview with an adult such as a parent, grandparent or friend of the family.

What to Do:
1) Prepare your subject in advance. Tell the person that you would like to have him or her tell a story about a time or event from the past that was important. Some topics might be:
   • how they came to this country or city
   • how they met their spouse
   • an adventure they once had
   • how a holiday such as Christmas, Passover or Canada Day was celebrated when they were children
   • how life was different when they were younger
2) Prepare yourself. Ask yourself what you already know about this person and what else you would like to know. Go to your interview with some questions to ask, questions that probe deeper into the person's past.
3) Listen carefully to the story and jot down simple notes. Or arrange to tape the interview and listen to the story again at your leisure.

What did you learn about the past? How is the past different from the present? What do you now know about your subject that you didn't know before?

4) Analyze your interviewing technique. Questioning and listening are the main ingredients to interviewing. How well did you listen? Did you ask probing questions, ones that checked the facts in the story, delved a little deeper, or prodded your subject into telling you a little more? How could you improve your technique?

DETECTIVE CHALLENGE: Aerial Photo Interpretation

Why not try your hand at reading the evidence provided by aerial photographs? Remember that changes in the landscape, slight shadows, and changes in plant growth may be evidence of something hidden underground.

First study the photographs below and write your own description and interpretation of what you see in each. Then look at the interpretations made by experienced archeologists shown on page 29 and try to match each one with the photo it relates to. Finally check the answers to see if you matched the photos correctly. How closely did your own first observations match the archeologists'?

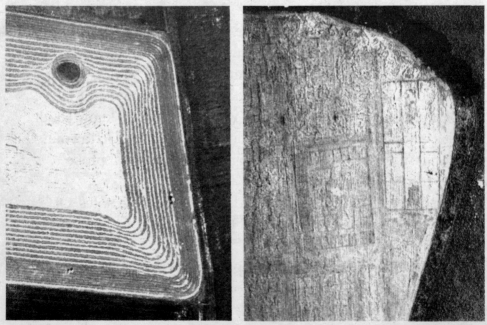

Figure 1

Dr. Georg Gerster, John Hillelson Agency

Figure 2

Figure 3

Arnold Baker

Figure 4

Chris Musson

Descriptions and Interpretations:

a) Description: slight rings or circular depressions in the ground.
   Interpretation: likely an enclosure or encampment that was once defended by a double ditch.

b) Description: abnormal growth pattern in a field of wheat.
   Interpretation: possibly the walls or foundations of a stone fortress lie buried beneath the soil.

c) Description: a small hill in a field of wheat.
   Interpretation: possibly a burial mound.

d) Description: flat mound surrounded by a deep gully or depression.
   Interpretation: probably the site of a castle or fortress that was surrounded by a deep moat.

Answers:
   a) Figure 4
   b) Figure 2
   c) Figure 1
   d) Figure 3

TIME PROBE: Undiscovered Site

In Search of Noah's Ark

Almost every culture around the globe passes stories from one generation to another. Many of the stories differ from tribe to tribe, from region to region. But one story bears striking similarities from one culture to another. It describes a great flood that wiped out almost every living thing on earth.

The Bible tells of such a great flood. In the Bible a man named Noah builds a massive ship or ark. Noah rounds up two of every species of animal living on earth, loads them on the Ark, then waits out a devastating rain storm that floods the entire earth. For forty days and nights the Ark is tossed and jostled like a cork on the swirling waves. Then finally the rains stop, the waters subside, and the Ark runs aground on a mountaintop.

Some people believe that the remains of such a vessel may lie on Mount Ararat, a mountain over five thousand metres tall in Turkey. One mountain climber claims to have seen a large flat-bottomed ship beneath a frozen lake near the peak of Mount Ararat. Another returned from a climb with a piece of black wood that dates back several thousand years. The wood does not come from trees that grow on or near the mountain, but from a region far away, an area the Bible identifies as Noah's homeland.

Evidence from Mount Ararat is sketchy at best. The top part of the mountain is continuously covered by ice. If a vessel such as the Ark exists, it is probably well hidden beneath tonnes of hardened snow. Finding any object under these conditions, even one as large as a ship, would be difficult. But such things are not impossible, as a recent discovery shows.

In 1991 two hikers spotted human bones poking through the crusty snow on a mountain in Italy. The hikers alerted scientists,

who uncovered the body of a 4000-year-old man. Excavation showed that the man wore tattered leather clothes and boots stuffed with straw insulation. He carried a bronze axe, a stone knife, a wooden backpack, and a small bag containing a flint for starting fires.

The man had likely been hiking on the mountain when he met with some accident. His body became covered by ice and snow, hidden from view, protected from decay, suspended in time. Then after thousands of years, the climate on the mountain began to change. Warmer, shorter winters caused the glacier to melt back, exposing the body and giving scientists an opportunity to study the frozen past.

Perhaps someday similar changes on Mount Ararat will unveil evidence of Noah's Ark.

4. GETTING SET TO DIG

The Case of THE VIKING PUZZLE

A thousand years ago a powerful people roamed the coasts of Northern Europe, exploring and conquering lands that lay in their path. These were the Vikings, a courageous and often ruthless seafaring group.

Stories of the Vikings have been told and retold over many centuries. Helge Ingstad, a Norwegian lawyer and explorer, and his wife Anne Stine Ingstad, an archeologist, had heard these Viking tales all their lives. They were enthralled by the Viking adventures, but one story in particular captured their imagination.

According to this story, on one of their tenth century voyages the Vikings stumbled upon a new land to the west of Greenland. It was a place of dense forests, fast-flowing streams and abundant wildlife. The Vikings established a colony in the new land and called it Vinland. For a few years the colony flourished. Then it was abruptly abandoned.

The Vinland tale was fascinating. If the story was true, Vinland must have been somewhere along the Atlantic coastline of North America. That would mean that Christopher Columbus was not the first European to visit the New World. The Vikings might have actually settled in North America almost five hundred years earlier!

But where was the proof? Where were the remains of this ancient settlement? Although archeologists had explored the Atlantic coastline, they had never found any signs of a Viking colony.

In the 1950s Helge Ingstad started to look into the Vinland story. He began by reading the earliest written records of the Viking voyages, a collection of stories known as the Sagas.

According to the Sagas the first Viking to reach the shores of North America was Bjarni Herjolfsson. While on a voyage from Iceland to Greenland in A.D. 986 Bjarni was driven off course by bad weather. He sailed much farther south than he expected, and as he

travelled back north he sighted three different and unfamiliar coasts. The first two were low-lying and forest-covered lands, but the third, the most northerly, was covered with mountains and glaciers. Bjarni did not land anywhere, but upon reaching Greenland he excitedly told of his find to anyone who would listen.

Bjarni's stories sparked the curiosity of another Viking, Leif Eriksson. Eriksson was a shrewd and adventurous man. He bought Bjarni's boat and, taking thirty-five men, set sail to see these lands for himself. He travelled south and came upon the glacier-covered, barren land described by Bjarni. He named it Helluland (Land of Flat Stones). The next land Leif encountered was covered with forests and white sandy beaches. He called this one Markland (Woodland). Finally after two more days of travel he reached the third place, the one Bjarni had seen first after being blown off course. That land was covered with forests and dotted with open stretches of grass. He named it Vinland.

The spot seemed ideal for a settlement. Leif and his crew built large houses and stayed the winter before returning to Greenland. When Leif's brothers and sister heard of the newly discovered lands they launched explorations of their own, bringing supplies and groups of men and women to live at Vinland. They erected other buildings and for several years harvested the timber and wildlife. Then suddenly Vinland was abandoned.

Helge Ingstad examined the Sagas for information about Vinland's location. Little by little he compiled a list of clues.

Clue: The Sagas said that it took Bjarni nine days to travel from Vinland back to Greenland. Viking ships were well built and the men were experienced sailors. On the average they could travel 240 kilometres a day. With this information Ingstad calculated that Vinland had to be roughly 2100 kilometres from Greenland.

Clue: The Sagas mentioned that even in the coldest months, day and night were almost equal in length at Vinland. Vinland couldn't be so far north that the days would be much shorter than nights in winter. Nor could it be so far south that the days would be much longer than nights.

Clue: The Vikings reported meeting a group of native people they called "Skraelings" at Vinland. The Skraelings used skin-covered boats for transportation. Native tribes along the Atlantic coast of Canada once used this style of craft, but tribes farther south did not.

Clue: In order to reach Vinland Leif Eriksson had sailed two days from Markland, a distance of some 500 kilometres. Markland was described as a flat land covered with wide sandy beaches and thick forests. To Ingstad that sounded like a description of the coast of Labrador, the mainland part of the province of Newfoundland. If Markland was Labrador, then Vinland was not far south.

There was only a narrow band of Atlantic coastline that seemed to fit all of these conditions. If the Sagas were accurate, Ingstad figured that Vinland had to be somewhere near the Maritime provinces of Canada.

Now that he had an idea of where to look, Ingstad needed to know what to look for. He re-read the Sagas again, this time searching for details of Vinland's appearance.

Clue: The Vikings reported landing at a place where a stream flowed out of a lake. There wide fields of grass and wheat were bordered by forests. Salmon filled the stream and berries grew wild in the area.

Clue: To reach Vinland Leif Eriksson sailed between an island in the north and a narrow jut of land in the south. Both landforms could be seen from the Vinland site.

Clue: To mark the site and to enable time and direction measurements to be taken, Leif and his men had piled stones into great heaps near the shoreline.

Armed with this information gleaned from the Sagas, Helge Ingstad set out to find Vinland. He started the search in Rhode Island in the United States, at the southern edge of the band of coastline he had identified earlier. For the next several summers he travelled northward along the Atlantic coast.

Ingstad travelled on foot and by bus, boat and plane. He kept searching for the features that had been described in the Sagas. Everywhere he asked the same question: "Have you seen any old ruins?" Sometimes he got a strange look as a reply. Sometimes he was treated with suspicion.

Then one day his routine question sparked a different response. "Yes, I seem to have heard about something like that," a villager in Newfoundland told him. Ingstad was led to a small town near the tip of the island of Newfoundland, the town of L'Anse aux Meadows.

As Ingstad stood at the shoreline an eerie feeling came over him. Although he had never been there before, it looked familiar. It seemed that the pages of the Sagas had suddenly come alive.

Nearby a cape of land jutted into the water. A large island loomed in the bay to the north. In the distance Ingstad could make out the hazy outline of the Labrador coast. A river flowed from a small lake, across grassy fields and into the bay. Salmon were abundant and wild berries hung from bushes everywhere.

A few hundred metres back Ingstad discovered large piles of rocks on a small hill. It looked as though the rocks had been stacked into towers. Perhaps they had once been used as markers to identify the spot. Or perhaps the rock towers had been used in some way to tell time.

For Ingstad the pieces of the puzzle fit. This was the place. Somewhere underneath this peaceful soil must lay the ruins of ancient Vinland.

But where to dig? Not far inland Ingstad noticed a few vague outlines on the ground that might suggest old buildings. Another possibility was revealed when sunlight reflected off the soil at just the right angle to outline straight shadowy ridges.

In the summer of 1961 the Ingstads returned to excavate at L'Anse aux Meadows. Anne Stine Ingstad headed the archeological team. The site was surveyed and mapped. A grid of stakes and string was constructed to divide the site into squares. One by one the squares were excavated.

Over three seasons of digging, the foundations of eight buildings were unearthed at L'Anse aux Meadows. Several were small dwellings, probably the living quarters of Viking families. Another was identified as a blacksmith shop. The largest building measured 21 metres long and 18 metres wide. It had been divided into six rooms, the largest being a type of great hall where the settlers likely gathered around a central fireplace to share meals and tales of their adventures.

No graves or skeletal remains were found. The acidic soil at the site had probably decomposed any organic matter centuries earlier. A few artifacts were located, among them a broken anvil, a few rusty nails and a soapstone spindle, part of an early spinning tool. Fourteen kilograms of iron bits were gathered from around the blacksmith shop. Ashes and charcoal were collected from cooking pits and fireplaces.

Evidence that this was the legendary Vinland site began to mount. Stone tools and flakes that are common on Indian or Eskimo sites were not found. The dwellings were built in the style and manner of Viking buildings found in Greenland. The metal pieces found at the site showed that the inhabitants were familiar with ways of extracting and using iron, something Vikings were able to do but native tribes of the time could not. In mid-winter the sun set around 4:30 P.M., making the day and night of almost equal length. When carbon 14 dating was done on the charcoal it pinpointed a date of A.D. 1060, plus or minus seventy years. This was well within the range of the Viking voyages.

An experiment conducted by Helge Ingstad provided additional proof of the site's identity. The Sagas reported a strange method of fishing that had been used at Vinland. Ingstad decided to try it out. He cut trenches parallel to the beach between the high and low tidemarks. At high tide the water swept into the trenches; at low tide it drained back. The trick worked. Ingstad found fish trapped in his trenches, exactly as the Vikings had a thousand years before.

The years spent probing for clues, then digging, researching and gathering evidence were not wasted. In the tradition of great detectives, the Ingstads were able to solve the mystery of the ancient Vikings. The site of Vinland was found at last.

NOTES: Preparing the Site

Once digging starts, the appearance of a site changes. Features such as hills, depressions, stones and surface artifacts disappear. Because the archeologist needs to know where objects were located even after they have been removed, careful records and maps of the site are needed.

One of the first tasks facing an archeologist when preparing a site map is the selection of a datum point. The datum point is a fixed spot at the site, usually some immovable feature such as a tree, a rock or a solidly planted stake. Even when the appearance of the site has changed, the datum point must remain. It is a reference spot for the archeologist. All boundaries, objects and directions on the archeologist's maps and records are identified in comparison to it.

Once a datum point is chosen, a topographical map is prepared. A topographical map shows hills, depressions and the location of objects on the surface such as buildings, streams, trees, rocks and foundations. By looking at this map the archeologist can tell exactly where these objects and landforms were positioned, their direction and distance from the datum point, and even their size and shape.

Next a grid is constructed. A grid is a system of lines similar to those found on graph paper. Using the datum point as a reference base, the site is divided into squares. Stakes are driven into the ground at each corner of the squares, and string is connected from one stake to another. Numbers and letters are written on the stakes to identify each square.

The grid is also plotted on a map using the same numbers and letters as on the stakes. Before any object is removed from the ground its location is plotted on this grid map, or on a similar map of a single square. In this way a complete record is kept of all artifacts.

Months or even years later the archeologist will be able to read the details of each artifact's location on maps and records from the site. The relative position of different artifacts and features will give the archeologist important information to help him understand the site's past.

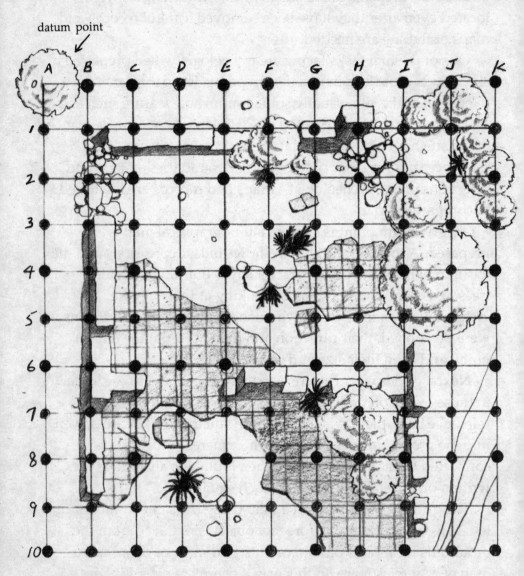

datum point

A B C D E F G H I J K

0
1
2
3
4
5
6
7
8
9
10

Topographical map and grid system

DETECTIVE CHALLENGE: Making a Top Plan

Each day a top plan of the grid square to be dug is made before work begins. The top plan is a sketch showing the square as it is seen from above. It shows features such as rocks, bones, differently coloured areas of soil, and artifacts that are currently visible on the surface of the square. The features are drawn to scale, with the size and position of each object accurately represented. The top plan provides a reference point, a record of the way things were before the day's digging started.

Why not try your hand at creating a top plan?

Materials:
- graph paper, or paper that you have ruled into 1 cm squares
- a variety of small objects that will fit on the graph paper such as pencils, erasers, small rocks, marbles, spoons, forks, paper clips, etc.
- a pencil, ruler and eraser

What to Do:
1) Place a sheet of graph paper on the floor.
2) Position the objects randomly on this sheet.
3) Take another sheet of graph paper. Stand over the objects so that you can see them from above. Sketch the objects on this paper. Be as precise as possible. Use the grid squares as a guide to ensure that the sizes and positions of the objects are accurate. When you are finished, your top plan should be a picture of the real objects as seen from above.
4) Check out how accurate you were. Give a blank sheet of graph paper and the same objects to someone else. Have your friend follow your top plan to position all the objects on the blank sheet. Does your friend's creation look like the original thing?

Digging Deeper:
Want to try a more advanced top plan? Grid squares at a dig site are large. A top plan that is the same size as the square would prove to be too large and awkward to handle. Instead a scale drawing is made. The scale drawing is accurate in all ways, but the square and the objects in it have been reduced in size.

The top plan becomes a miniature replica of the actual square.

You can make a scale version of a top plan by following these steps.

1) Place your objects on top of a full sheet of graph paper as before.

2) Take a blank sheet of graph paper. Fold it in half, then fold it in half again. Open the paper. You should see four sections. Cut out the sections.

3) On one of the cut-out sections, draw a top plan of the objects. Because you have half the number of squares along the length and half the number of squares along the width, your drawing will be reduced in size by half. We say that the plan is drawn to a scale of 1:2.

An example may help you do your sketch. If an object on the full size graph paper is located ten squares from the left side and six squares from the bottom, you would sketch it in half as far on the top plan — five squares from the left and three squares from the bottom. If the object is twenty squares long on the original, it will be only half as long on the top plan — ten squares in length. All dimensions are reduced by half.

4) Again test your top plan. Give it and the objects to a volunteer and have him or her recreate the original on a blank sheet of full size graph paper. How well did you both do?

DETECTIVE CHALLENGE: Tools of the Trade

What kinds of tools does a detective of time use on a dig? Bulldozers? Picks and axes? Shovels?

Not usually. The work of archeology has to proceed slowly and cautiously. In order to preserve the evidence, small tools are needed. Most archeologists carry these tools to the site in a packsack or bag.

You would recognize most of the tools. Many of them are items that you have in the garage, kitchen or bathroom of your home. An archeologist simply uses them in a different way.

Below is a photograph of the objects taken out of one of these packs. Can you identify what each of the tools is? Can you guess how each is used at the dig site? Compare your guesses with the answers that follow.

THE DETECTIVE OF TIME PACKSACK:

Photo by: Paul Heersink

ANSWERS:

trowel: for scraping away the soil and lowering the surface evenly

tweezers: for picking up small items

aluminum foil: for wrapping datable materials such as shells, charcoal, etc.

toothbrush: for scrubbing artifacts and bones

styrofoam pad: for kneeling on while digging to prevent contact with the cold, damp earth

knife: for scraping and prying objects from the soil

measuring tape: for locating stakes and taking measurements

small bags: for storing objects taken from the site

pencil and notebook: for keeping records of the excavation

paintbrush: for sweeping away dirt from around bones and artifacts

compass: for laying out the site and checking the location afterwards

pruning shears: for snipping roots that interfere with digging

TIME PROBE: Ancient Legend

On the Trail of King Arthur

Legend holds that during the sixth century A.D. a king named Arthur ruled Britain. Arthur was handsome and brave, a man capable of inspiring and leading others. He gathered a band of 150 knights around him, swore them to a code of loyalty and honesty, and fought to rid Britain of evil and wrongdoing. Because the knights met regularly with Arthur around a round table in his home at Camelot, the group became known as the Knights of the Round Table.

As legend has it, Arthur and his knights united Britain and brought an era of peace to the land. After a long reign Arthur died. His body was secretly buried in a tomb beneath a monastery on an island known as the Isle of Avalon.

Today no Camelot or Isle of Avalon graces the map of Britain. These places, if ever they existed, have vanished over time. There are, however, dozens of modern day places that claim some connection to the legendary king. By checking historical records and dating artifacts, archeologists have been able to eliminate many of these as possible sites.

For example, a castle in Cornwall holds that it is the birthplace of Arthur. But the castle was built in the thirteenth century, 700 years after Arthur's time. In another case, a circular table is displayed in a castle in Winchester. Above the table hangs a painting of Arthur seated on a throne, sceptre in hand. Many claim that the table is Arthur's Round Table, but again the time periods do not fit. The tabletop dates to the twelfth century, the painting to the sixteenth century.

Is the Arthur story merely fancy, not fact? Was there ever a King Arthur? A kingdom such as Camelot? And if so, where is the proof?

In the 1960s an interesting discovery was made at South Cadbury in southwestern England. Beneath the flat summit of a small hill archeologists found the remains of a large fort from about 500 A.D. It was once protected by circular rises of earth and stone. Not far away, at the monastery of Glastonbury, monks in the twelfth century claimed to have located a tomb containing human bones and a cross with the name Arthur on it. These artifacts, if they ever existed, have long since disappeared. But archeologists digging in the ruins of the monastery not long ago did discover an empty tomb that may be the same one.

Could these be the sites of Camelot and the burial place of Arthur, the valiant king? Because no definite evidence of Arthur has been found at South Cadbury it is impossible to be sure.

But one convincing piece of evidence does add weight to the claim. Glastonbury is now surrounded by dry land, but at one time — as far back as the sixth century — it was an island. An island surrounded by marsh.

The Isle of Avalon perhaps?

Time may tell.

5. EXCAVATING A SITE

The Case of THE HOT SPRINGS GRAVE

For decades visitors have come to the town of Hot Springs, South Dakota to bask in its natural warm-water springs. Now over 50 000 people a year come for another reason — to view a spectacle thousands of years in the making, yet only recently discovered by accident.

In June 1974 workers started to prepare some land on the southeast side of Hot Springs for a new housing development. Heavy equipment operator George Hanson climbed aboard his bulldozer, started the engine, and aimed its blade at a small hill. The bulldozer sliced through the soil, carving a deep gouge in the hillside. Suddenly the blade scraped against something hard. A strip of white gleamed in the red soil.

Curious, Hanson stopped his machine and climbed down for a closer look. He saw a two-metre-long tusk sliced lengthwise by the bulldozer blade. Scattered around it were other bones.

Hanson gathered some of the bones and took them home. He showed them to his son Dan, who had studied geology and archeology. When Dan realized that these were not ordinary bones he phoned his university professor to come and look at the site. He even staked out the bulldozed area and kept a 24-hour watch over it so nothing could disturb the find.

The Hot Springs site proved to be one of the most promising paleontological finds ever. Paleontology is the study of animals and plants that existed before the time of humans. The Hot Springs bones were mammoth bones, the remains of giant elephant-like prehistoric animals. A quick analysis of the uncovered bones revealed that they were from at least eight separate mammoths. Who could tell how many more were hidden in the soil!

Over the next few years scientists and their volunteer helpers probed the hill with shovels, scrapers, trowels and brushes. Although the work is not yet completed, the bones of more than forty mammoths have already been found in the Hot Springs hill, making it one of the most concentrated sites of mammoth bones in the world.

A single mammoth skeleton is an unusual find, but to discover a whole cluster of skeletons in one location is extremely rare. That puzzled scientists and raised many questions. How did so many mammoths become buried in one spot? How did they die?

During the excavation of a site every sample of bone and soil taken is considered to be a clue. Many kinds of evidence have been gathered from the Hot Springs site. Taken separately the samples do not solve the mystery of the mammoths. But taken together the clues give a clearer understanding of what happened long ago.

Rock samples from the area around the mammoth site show that it was surrounded by shale, a type of rock formed when sediments of sand, silt and mud harden. The area of the site itself was once an oval-shaped pit about 45 metres across.

Along with mammoth remains, specimens from animals such as minnows, frogs, snails and clams have been found at the site. This means that the pit was once filled with warm, spring-fed water, with lush vegetation growing around it. Because shale is soft and easily eroded, the banks of the pit would have been slippery, steep and fragile. Over time more and more of the sides would have collapsed into the water, making the pit a giant sinkhole.

Skeletal remains of mice, prairie dogs, squirrels and other small land animals have also been found. They suggest that the surrounding area was once grassland or prairie and that trees were sparse. Fossil pollen samples also taken from the site support this idea.

Special dating tests on mammoth bone samples show that the animals died about 26 000 years ago. No evidence of man has been found at the site, and humans probably did not even arrive in the area until many years later, so the mammoths were not slaughtered by hunters.

Bones found at the site show that the mammoths were almost

five metres tall. Impressions of mammoth toeprints have been found pressed into the floor of the sinkhole. This suggests that the water was likely about five metres deep and that some animals tried to keep their heads above water by walking on tiptoe.

When the bones recovered from the site were marked on a map of the pit, an interesting pattern developed. Most of the mammoth bones were found within six metres of the sinkhole edge. Few have been found in the centre. It seems that most of the mammoths died trying to climb out of the watery trap.

Putting all these and other clues together, it is possible to recreate the scene at the sinkhole as it must have happened thousands of years ago . . .

● ● ●

Water! That's what the mammoth needed. After munching on tender grasses for so long, the gigantic animal was thirsty. Ahead an inviting pond offered relief.

Almost five metres tall, the mammoth lumbered towards the banks of the pond, its ten tonnes shifting slowly from side to side. The animal stooped low. Dipping its trunk into the refreshing water, it satisfied its thirst.

Suddenly the bank gave way and the mammoth plunged into the water. Alarmed, it struggled to its feet and tried to climb back up the

bank. But the red shale was slippery and steep. Under the weight of the mammoth the soil crumbled, slipping into the pond like a mudslide.

Again and again the mammoth tried to scale the bank, but the sides were too steep, too slippery, too fragile. The animal was trapped.

All day and night the mammoth continued to struggle. Its frantic trumpeting filled the air. But by morning the huge beast was exhausted. Too tired to struggle, unable to keep its head above water, the mammoth sank to the bottom, where warm water sealed its fate. Churned by an underground spring, mud and sand gradually settled like dust over the body, eventually covering it completely.

● ● ●

Over a 300- to 700-year period many other mammoths ventured into the same watery trap, only to die of drowning or starvation. Smaller animals wandered into the pit too. They suffered a similar fate.

Eventually the pool dried up. Layers of sand and mud hardened, protecting the animal remains. Over thousands of years the softer surrounding shale eroded more quickly than the deposits. The pond area eventually became a hill, a giant graveyard awaiting discovery.

Today a large research and visitor centre covers the sinkhole area. Visitors walk along specially constructed paths. They can view prehistoric remains that have been left exactly as they were originally uncovered. On each side of the path scientists continue their excavations.

So far more than 80 tusks and 640 bones have been uncovered. Along with these remains of more than forty mammoths, other prehistoric animals such as an extinct breed of camel, the pig-like peccary, and the rare giant short-faced bear have been exposed.

But only a small part of the hill has been unearthed. Over the next decade more soil will be carefully etched away, and more of nature's 26 000-year-old life and death drama will be revealed.

NOTES: Excavating the Site

Courtesy of the Royal Ontario Museum, Toronto, Canada

Once a site has been researched, surveyed, mapped and marked with string and stakes, excavation can begin.

But where will the digging start? The methods described in Chapter 3 for locating a site are also used to pinpoint likely squares. A probe trench or test pit may be dug through part of the site to give a better understanding of what lies below. At other times the choice of squares is made randomly, so every square has an equal chance of being dug.

Workers are assigned to individual squares. First the worker searches the surface for artifacts. A top plan is made to show the position of each object on the ground. Then any artifacts are placed in bags labelled with the square location. The square location is the set of numbers and letters that corresponds to those marked on the grid map and the stakes at the corner of the square.

Once surface material has been removed, small tools such as hand picks and trowels are used to gradually loosen and scrape away the soil in thin layers. Loosened soil is scooped into a bucket. When the bucket is full the worker carries it to another location where it is spread on a fine mesh screen and shaken through or washed through with a stream of water. The screen filters out small objects such as beads, broken fragments of artifacts, and tiny bones, which can add valuable information to an excavation.

Work proceeds carefully and slowly. Sometimes the surface is lowered only a few centimetres in a day. When the worker comes across something significant in the soil, even greater care is taken.

An artifact or bone embedded in the soil is gradually exposed

using picks, spoons and small brushes. Before it is removed, it is photographed and notes about its location, size and condition are recorded in a field book. A sketch of the square showing its exact location is also included.

If an object is in good condition, it may be gently pried loose and placed in a bag labelled with its location and depth. If it is in poor condition, it may have to be treated before it is moved to prevent damage. If it is fragile, some of the surrounding soil may be removed with it to provide extra support. Alternatively, it may be encased in plaster to protect it when it is moved.

Artifacts are not the only significant things found in squares. Differences in the colour of the soil can often be important. They may indicate that a pit, post or fire was once present in a particular spot. Like artifacts, such features are recorded in the field book and on the map.

Differences in soil also mark different layers. For this reason the sides of a square are also carefully charted. Diagrams of the layers encountered as a square becomes deeper can help archeologists identify different periods during the history of a site. Sometimes baulks or narrow walls are left between squares to maintain a record of these layers.

Samples of a variety of materials are taken during an excavation. Soil, rock and charcoal samples can all provide information about a site's past. Soil and rock samples help to determine the geography of the site when it was in use. Pollen found in soil samples tells scientists about the vegetation of the area. Charcoal samples can be used to pinpoint dates.

Weeks, months and even years may be spent unearthing a

single site. The work proceeds slowly, square by square. With each discovery questions are posed, new information is compiled, and more pieces of the puzzling past are assembled.

DETECTIVE CHALLENGE: Making and Using Plaster Casts

Sometimes an archeologist or paleontologist finds only an imprint of an object rather than the object itself. To recreate the features of the original, a plaster cast is often made.

The plaster casts made in Pompeii are a good example. When the Italian city was destroyed by a volcanic eruption in A.D. 79, many people and animals were killed in the disaster. The hot wet ash from the explosion settled over the bodies, then cooled and hardened. Although the bodies themselves have disappeared over time, hardened moulds of volcanic ash have taken their place. By pouring plaster into the moulds, archeologists have been able to make plaster replicas of the victims. These plaster casts have helped scientists understand more about the disaster and its effect on the communities near the volcano.

An imprint is located under the surface.

A hole is drilled from the surface into the imprint space.

The space is filled with wet plaster.

The surrounding material is removed, exposing the hardened plaster.

Here is a recipe for plaster of Paris. Following it are two activities that will show you how plaster of Paris works and how you can use it to collect and identify evidence.

Recipe for Plaster of Paris:

Materials:
- plaster of Paris powder, obtainable from hardware stores
- a small plastic container for mixing
- a stick or spoon for stirring
- a measuring cup
- a container of cold water

What to Do:
1) Measure 125 ml (½ cup) of cold water and pour it into the mixing container.
2) Measure 125 ml (½ cup) of plaster of Paris. Add it to the cold water.
3) Stir thoroughly with the stick or spoon. Properly mixed plaster of Paris should be the consistency of paint or heavy cream. If your batch is too watery, add a tiny bit more plaster of Paris. If it is too thick, add a little water.

I. Making Plaster Casts
Materials:
- one batch of plaster of Paris, mixed just before it is needed
- clay or Plasticine
- margarine container
- baby powder or talc
- objects to make imprints of, such as screws, nuts, shells, pencils, coins etc.

What to Do:
1) Roll out the clay or Plasticine into a flat slab 2 cm thick. Cut and shape a piece of the slab to fit the bottom of the margarine container.
2) Sprinkle talc or baby powder on the objects you wish to cast

and on the slab in the container. This makes it easier to remove the objects later.

3) Press each object into the slab, then remove it carefully.

4) Mix the plaster of Paris following the directions in the recipe.

5) Pour the mixture over the slab in the container.

6) When the plaster is firm to the touch, pry the cast carefully from the slab. Compare your plaster copy to the original objects. Did your plaster of Paris make identifiable casts? Show your casts to someone else to see if he or she can identify the objects correctly.

II. Collecting and Identifying Prints

Materials:
- plaster of Paris powder (premeasured and stored in a plastic bag)
- water (stored in a sealed plastic container)
- strips of stiff paper, 4 cm wide and at least 30 cm long
- paper clips

What to Do:

1) Search outdoors for animal tracks, footprints or other imprints in the soil such as the tire tracks of a car.

2) Make a circle of one paper strip and hold it together with a paper clip.

3) Centre the paper circle around the footprint or track on the ground.

4) Mix the plaster and pour it over the print.

5) Wait until the plaster hardens, then pry it loose and remove the paper strip from around it. Your plaster cast should be a replica of the object which made the original print.

6) Try to identify the print. Who or what made it? Use reference books to match casts of animal tracks with the animals that made them. Examine the tread patterns on casts of footprints and tire tracks. Try to identify the shoes or tires that made the prints.

TIME PROBE: Legend Confirmed?

The Story of Atlantis: Fact or Fiction?

Imagine an island, lush and green. It is blessed with magnificent mountain ranges, sweeping plains and luxuriant gardens. Exotic animals roam the countryside. The land is rich with precious stones and rare metals.

An intelligent, peaceful people inhabits this island. They have built a beautiful city designed in alternating circles of land and water around a huge gold- and silver-topped palace. They live in quiet harmony with each other and their environment. Crime is almost non-existent. Laws are barely needed. The people are content, fulfilled, prosperous.

Is such a paradise possible?

According to Plato, a Greek philosopher who wrote in the fourth century B.C., a kingdom matching this description once existed. That land was called Atlantis.

Atlantis was located in the Atlantic Ocean just west of the Straits of Gibraltar, the narrow channel of water that separates Spain from Africa. It was a place of tremendous beauty, the centre of power and wisdom in the ancient world. But as Plato tells the story, the civilization of Atlantis came to a tragic and sudden end.

As time passed the people of Atlantis became greedy, wanting more power, more possessions. They ventured to other lands, where they attacked and ransacked other cities. These actions offended the gods. In retribution for the wrongdoings, the gods hurled destruction upon the island: "There occurred violent earthquakes and floods, and in a single day and night of rain . . . the island of Atlantis . . . disappeared and was sunk beneath the sea."

Plato's description of the mystical civilization of Atlantis has prompted numerous searches for the lost land. Claims that Atlantis has been rediscovered have been made frequently, and thousands of books have been written on the subject.

Was there ever a real Atlantis?

The answer to this question may lie among a cluster of three small islands that surround a circular basin of water in the Mediterranean Sea about 120 kilometres north of Crete.

The largest of the islands, Thira (Santorini), is covered in a blanket of pumice and volcanic ash. Thira is crescent-shaped and has an unusual shoreline. The inside of the crescent wraps itself around the central basin, with 300-metre-high cliffs that soar above the water and plunge sharply into the sea. The outside of the crescent, however, has a shore that slopes gently and easily into the Mediterranean. The circular basin itself is so deep that ships cannot anchor in it.

In 1967 Greek archeologist Spyridon Marinatos found an ancient city buried beneath 30 metres of ash on the south end of Thira. Although the city's palace, temple and other structures had been destroyed, the elegance of the past showed through their ruins. Marinatos and his workers unearthed pottery, statues, woven baskets and other delicate objects.

But it was the frescoes or paintings on the walls that best depicted life as it must have been long ago. One painting showed groups of antelope, another a troop of blue monkeys of a species now found only in Africa. A third fresco showed a quiet island scene complete with clusters of birds and flowers. The residents of this city seem to have been civilized, at one with nature, at peace with themselves.

Scientists believe that life on the island ended suddenly. Their studies of the collapsed walls of the city, the artifacts buried beneath, the heavy layer of volcanic ash, and the unusual shapes of the island and its basin have revealed that at one time the three small islands were part of a larger one. A volcanic mountain stood at its centre surrounded by rich soil and lush forests. A city grew along its southern shore.

Then one day 3 500 years ago the volcano exploded with the force of a thousand atomic bombs. The blast echoed from one end of the Mediterranean to the other. Molten pumice and hot ash spewed into the sky, blotting out the sun, turning day into night. The great volcano collapsed upon itself, forming a crater 11 kilometres across. Sea water gushed into the pit. Churned by the explosion, tidal waves 200 metres high smashed along coastlines, sweeping away towns and villages.

In one day the city and most of the mountain island were gone, erased from time by a single disaster. Only fragments remained —three small islands around a circular basin, toppled stone structures smothered beneath a blanket of ash, hidden relics of an earlier time.

Is it possible that this disaster was the basis for Plato's story? Could the island of Thira have been the fabled Atlantis? Or was Atlantis Crete, whose rich Minoan civilization may have been destroyed by the same explosion (see *The Case of the Monster and the Maze*)?

Although excavations still continue, many scholars believe that the discoveries at Thira do explain the story of Atlantis. After the explosion the tale of such a major tragedy was undoubtedly passed from generation to generation, the details changing with each retelling. Dates, descriptions, even locations may have been altered. Perhaps Plato, writing a thousand years after the disaster, could have heard and recorded a story mixed with fact and fiction.

Or was Plato writing about something totally unrelated to Thira? The final decision about Atlantis — if one is possible — still waits for future scholars to unravel it.

6. SEARCHING UNDERWATER

The Case of THE KING'S WARSHIP

• • •

Sunday, August 10, 1628.

A proud day for Sweden.

After months of preparation, King Gustaf II Adolf's newest and most splendid warship, the Vasa, stands ready to be launched in Stockholm harbour.

Little expense has been spared to build the 1400 tonne galleon. Only the finest materials have been used — thick oak for the hull, deck and masts; gold gilding for the carved lion figurehead; heavy bronze for the gleaming cannon.

The Vasa is a giant, over 60 metres long and 30 metres tall. Dozens of sails, large and small, stand ready to catch the slightest breeze.

Designed for battle, the ship has 64 gunports arranged in two tiers. Normally a door seals each gunport, preventing water from entering, but also hiding the cannon from enemy view. Today for the launching ceremonies, the gunports are open, the cannon proudly on display.

Seamen unfurl the sails and cast off the moorings. A cheer rises from the waiting crowd as a light southwest breeze ripples the canvas. Slowly the Vasa eases away from her berth and heads for open water.

The pride of the royal navy slices majestically across the harbour. In minutes the Vasa nears an island over a kilometre from the quay.

Then a sudden gust of wind catches the sails. The Vasa leans awkwardly to one side. The sailors pause, expecting the ship to right herself, but in the wind she leans further. At this angle the lower gunports dip below the waterline. Water gushes through the openings, tipping the vessel even further.

The crowd on shore gasps, their cheers strangled by disbelief. In a matter of minutes the impossible happens — the Vasa sinks to the muddy bottom of Stockholm harbour and 50 lives are lost.

• • •

In the decades that followed the sinking of the *Vasa*, several attempts were made to salvage the ship. In one effort lines were attached to the masts and horses on shore hauled the ship upright. In another attempt hooks, tongs and grapnels were dragged through the water, ripping open the upper deck. Then divers used an odd-shaped diving bell to recover more than 50 of the cannons.

But most of the attempts were futile. By 1670 all efforts to salvage the *Vasa* had ceased. The king's ship rested undisturbed on the muddy bottom of the harbour, its location becoming lost in the sweep of time until, centuries later, a Swedish citizen picked up the trail of clues.

Anders Franzen had always been fascinated by the sea. As a child he listened closely to tales of shipwrecks and sea battles told by his father. He spent summer vacations looking for watery finds. While other children played games, Franzen dived into the waters off Sweden's coast or dragged a grapnel from a boat, hoping to snag pieces of wreckage.

Even later when he became a petroleum engineer Franzen maintained his interest in shipwrecks. In 1939 he came to an important realization while vacationing off the west coast of Sweden. He found some waterlogged timber that was riddled with holes, the destructive work of the teredo, a type of shipworm. Timber retrieved from the south and east coasts of Sweden, he noted, was not damaged in that way. The coldness of those waters and their low salt content made the teredo inactive. In those waters wooden wrecks were much more apt to be intact, free of holes and decay.

Franzen decided to narrow his search for a wrecked ship to the Baltic Sea on the east coast of Sweden. He pored over research material, reading and rereading historical records in museums and government archives.

The lavishly decorated wooden warships of the sixteenth and seventeenth centuries appealed to him most. He made a list of about 50 ships from this time period that were known to have been wrecked off Sweden's east coast. Then he narrowed the list down to a dozen.

The *Vasa* soon topped Franzen's list. It was one of the largest and most richly decorated of all the missing ships. Furthermore, because it was made of sturdy oak, had sunk within minutes and had been pulled upright in early salvage attempts, the *Vasa* stood a good chance of still being intact.

By 1954 Franzen had collected a great deal of information about the *Vasa*. He mapped its possible locations and began a systematic search of the harbour. Using borrowed or rented boats, he spent every Saturday and Sunday for the next three summers dragging the bottom with grapnels and wire hooks. To the amusement of curious harbour crews he hauled old tires, stoves, bedframes and even discarded Christmas trees from the water. But evidence of the *Vasa* eluded him.

Then in 1956 Franzen examined an engineers' report for a proposed bridge across the harbour. On a contour map of the harbour bottom he noticed an unusual hump near the island of Beckholmen. Could this be the *Vasa*? The hump was only a heap of rubble, he was told, a pile of rock deposited in the harbour during the construction of a dock years before.

But Franzen was skeptical. He returned to the archives to reread early government records about the *Vasa*. Key words now leaped at him from a yellowed piece of paper dated August 12, 1628: "She came out into the bay . . . more wind into her sails . . . Beckholmen . . . fell on her side and sank in 18 fathoms of water . . ."

Beckholmen! The hump on the contour map!

Franzen wasted no time. He gathered maps, grapnels and a curious new instrument he had invented himself — a marine core sampler. Made of steel, weighing almost three kilograms, and shaped like a cylinder with a pointed hollow end, the core sampler enabled Franzen to reel in small samples of debris from the harbour floor.

Using the contour map as a guide, Franzen anchored off Beckholmen. He dropped the core sampler overboard, waited until it struck bottom, then eagerly hauled it up. Wedged in the hollow point he found a chunk of black wood — a plug of aged oak. Again and again he dropped the core sampler overboard,

58

covering wider and wider areas. Each time he hauled up a plug of blackened oak.

Naval divers were soon enlisted to explore the muddy bottom. Wearing a helmet and hoses and armed with a telephone, the first diver plunged into the water while Franzen waited above.

In a short time Franzen heard an excited cry. "Wait a minute! I just reached out and touched something solid . . . it feels like a wall of wood! It's a big ship, all right!"

The *Vasa* at last!

The wreck rested upright under thirty-three metres of water, its hull wedged in thick mud. Beneath the blackened oak and layers of silt, the beauty of the original vessel was obvious. Despite three centuries under water and damage from early salvage attempts, the *Vasa* was in remarkable condition.

Under ordinary circumstances a ship such as the *Vasa* would be studied below water. Excavation methods used on land are adapted for use underwater. A vessel is surveyed, measured and photographed. A grid is constructed, and artifacts charted and plotted as they are uncovered. Then they are brought to the surface to be catalogued, preserved and studied.

Because of the *Vasa*'s excellent condition, however, a bold new scheme was suggested. Why not raise the entire ship out of the water?

Plans for seventeenth century ships were scarce, so scientists knew little about vessels of that period. Builders of the time had worked from simple sketches and kept shipbuilding secrets to themselves. Without written records much had been lost. If the *Vasa* could be brought out of the water, methods and materials of the past could be studied firsthand.

A three-stage plan for lifting, preserving and restoring the ship was developed. In the first stage the *Vasa* would be moved closer to shore. Divers drilled holes into the harbour bottom on each side of the ship, then connected them with tunnels that passed under the hull. Thick steel cables were threaded through the tunnels and attached to two large pontoons, one on either side of the ship.

Even this early in the salvage operation the *Vasa* began to release its treasures. Divers found elaborate carvings as they worked in the mud — lions, mermaids, Greek gods and goddesses, shields bearing the royal coats of arms. Debris from around the ship was pumped to the surface and sifted to locate smaller artifacts.

By August 1959 all was ready. Water was drained from the pontoons. As they grew more buoyant the pontoons inched upwards, prying the *Vasa* from the muddy bottom. Still submerged and hovering just above the harbour floor, the vessel was slowly towed landward until its hull gently scraped bottom. Then the process of lifting, towing and grounding was repeated several times. With each move the *Vasa* edged closer to shore. By September the ship lay submerged in only 15 metres of water.

In the second stage of salvage two problems were tackled. Between 1959 and 1961 divers boarded up the gunports, repaired the deck and hull, and made the *Vasa* as watertight as possible. At the same time restoration crews experimented with ways of preserving the fragile craft and its contents.

In the final and most delicate stage hydraulic jacks were fastened to the sides of the two pontoons. Additional cables were passed under the hull and attached to the jacks. Then four inflatable rubber pontoons were fixed to the hull to add more buoyancy.

Finally the rubber pontoons were inflated. At the same time the jacks began to haul in the wire. Carefully the *Vasa* was lifted to the surface. Powerful pumps emptied the water out of the craft, enabling the *Vasa* to remain afloat for the first time in 333 years.

On May 4, 1961, the ship was towed to Beckholmen. After being set on a concrete drydock, the *Vasa* was soaked with a constant stream of water to prevent it from drying out and deteriorating. Plastic film was wrapped around portions of the vessel to conserve moisture. Finally all wooden parts were sprayed continuously for months with polyethylene glycol, a waxy substance that forces out moisture while strengthening the wood.

Franzen and his archeological team found that there was more to the *Vasa* than just its decorated shell. Inside the ship they located dishes, pieces of money and clothing, weapons, tools, powder kegs, even barrels of butter. Twelve skeletons of drowned sailors lay among the cannons. The vessel proved to be rich in fascinating detail that told much about the habits and dress of the time.

Photo by: Max Lewold

After being preserved, investigated and restored, the *Vasa* was placed on display for the public. Today King Gustaf's warship and many of the artifacts found in it can be seen in the *Vasa* Museum in Stockholm.

DETECTIVE FILE # 6

NOTES: Underwater Archeology

A land archeologist and an underwater archeologist do many of the same things. But because the underwater archeologist works below water, many of the tasks must be approached differently.

On land the archeologist looks for visible signs of a promising site. Depressions in the ground, mounds, unusual plant growth, artifacts on the surface — all of these are signs of hidden ruins.

In the water things are not so simple. Visible signs are trapped beneath a blanket of water and are often covered with sediment or plant growth. To see them first-hand the archeologist must dive to the bottom using scuba gear or a diving suit. For safety reasons a diver cannot remain underwater for more than a few hours a day. An archeological search done this way is therefore slow and tedious.

To overcome the limitations of this kind of search the underwater archeologist often relies on scientific equipment and techniques similar to those used on land. They allow the archeologist to survey the bottom from above the water rather than under it.

One of the most important techniques is called sonar. Sonar is short for "sound navigation and ranging." When sonar equipment is used a beam of sound is sent from the ship through the water. This beam bounces off solid objects and returns to the ship as an echo. Electronic equipment on the ship processes the echo and gives the archeologist important information about the depth of the water, the material on the bottom, and any unusual or large shapes that might be there.

Television can be used to substitute for the human eye. Cameras lowered into the water and towed by cable send pictures of the bottom back to the ship. Making video recordings of such an underwater search allows the archeologist to replay and analyze the scene as often as necessary.

A sensitive type of metal detector is sometimes used in an underwater search. The sensing device is towed through the water by cable, sending electronic signals to a processing unit aboard the ship. By monitoring the signals, small metal objects can be detected at great distances.

Once a promising site is found, samples from the bottom may be taken. A coring device like the one developed by Franzen to locate the *Vasa* is sometimes used to bring up bits of debris and wreckage from the ocean floor.

When the site has been pinpointed, divers may be asked to do a careful visual survey of the area. But if the ruins are located at a great depth, too deep for extended exploration by divers, the archeologist may rely on another technological innovation — a small one or two person submarine. Armed with searchlights, cameras and even sometimes radio-controlled robots, a small submarine permits the researcher to survey the site first-hand without even getting wet.

As with surface digs, an underwater site must be prepared

before excavation can begin. A grid, usually made of brightly painted metal pipes or coloured cables, is laid over the site. Sometimes the grid is anchored on the ocean floor; other times it is suspended from floats above the ruins. The position of each find can be precisely recorded using this grid.

Much underwater excavation can be done using just the diver's hand to fan away covering sediment. But sometimes artifacts are deeply covered. In that case the underwater archeologist needs special tools to help with excavation and recovery. The jet hose is a hose that shoots out pressurized water with such force that it cuts away layers of sediment on the ocean floor to expose underlying artifacts. The airlift is a sort of high-power vacuum cleaner that sucks up mud and sand and sends it to the ship. There the sediment is screened for small objects just as it is on land.

Artifacts which are found at an underwater site are mapped and drawn or photographed before being moved. Smaller pieces are then collected with pincers and a bucket and taken directly to the surface by the diver. Larger objects are sometimes raised with the help of cables, winches and flotation bags. As in surface excavations, all objects are carefully cleaned, catalogued, restored and studied in the lab.

DETECTIVE CHALLENGE: Screening for Artifacts

How good a detective are you? Could you find a needle in a haystack? How about a tiny fish bone in a mound of dirt?

Objects from the past come in all sizes. Some, like the fish bone, are so small that locating them is a little like finding a needle in a haystack. No matter what its size, however, each of these objects is a clue, a bit of evidence that an archeologist shouldn't miss.

To increase the chances of finding such small objects, archeologists usually screen the dirt or sediment that they remove from a site. Fine particles of sand, soil or silt will pass through a screen, but larger objects won't.

Try your own hand at such small-scale detection.

Materials:

- two buckets or large jars
- a mixture of sand, soil, small stones and pebbles
- some small objects: beads, buttons, marbles, nails, tiny screws, etc.
- a fine mesh screening material such as window screening or cheesecloth
- string or elastics

What to Do:

1) Prepare your materials. Put the sand, soil, stone and pebbles in the bucket or jar. Add water to make a soupy mixture.

2) Select several of the small objects, put them in the bucket or jar, and mix or shake well. If you want to add more mystery to this activity, ask someone else to secretly select some of the objects and put them into the bucket.

3) Stretch the screen or cheesecloth over another bucket or jar. Wrap elastic bands or tie string around the material to hold it in place.

4) This next step is messy, so it is best done outdoors or over newspaper. Slowly and carefully pour some of the mixture through the screen. Do little bits at a time. Let the liquid drain, then examine the residue for artifacts.

How good a detective were you? Did you find all of the objects?

TIME PROBE: The Past Submerged

Finding El Dorado

When Spanish explorers first trekked across South America they heard a marvellous tale from native Indians. The story told of a sacred mountain lake in Columbia and a chief named El Dorado — the Golden Man.

According to the story the natives believed that Lake Guatavita was home to the sun god. To please the god, El Dorado and his subjects gathered at the lake once each year. The chief covered his body with sticky gum and his followers blew gold dust on him until he shone like the sun. Then El Dorado was rowed out to the middle of the lake on a specially constructed raft. There he dove into the water to wash the gold off his body, while his followers hurled other golden treasures into the lake as tribute.

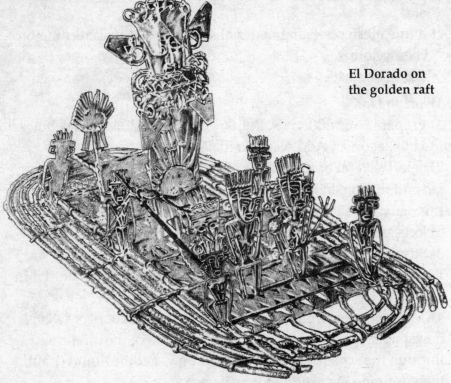

El Dorado on the golden raft

The tale of El Dorado has captured the imagination of many adventurers. In 1580 a wealthy Spanish merchant organized eight thousand Indian workers to cut a deep channel into the lake. By draining water through the channel, the level of the lake was dropped significantly and the muddy shore was exposed. A few gold objects were recovered, but mud and rock plugged the channel again. Before the merchant could start a new expedition he died, so the project was abandoned.

Earlier this century a British company made another attempt to drain the lake, this time by drilling a tunnel to lower the water level. Because the mud on the exposed lake floor was too soft and deep to walk on, the workers decided to let it harden in the hot sun. By the time the expedition resumed, the baked mud had blocked the drainage tunnel and rain had filled the lake again.

Numerous failed attempts like these have raised doubts about the El Dorado story. Was there ever really a Golden Man? A sacred lake? Or, like other legends, had this one grown with each telling until fact and fiction were impossible to distinguish?

A 1969 discovery hints that the El Dorado story may indeed be based on fact. Two farmers exploring a cave near Bogata, Columbia, found a golden model of a raft. Small human figures ride the miniature craft. At the centre sits a golden man on a throne. Around him, facing outward, sit eight oarsmen.

If Lake Guatavita is the sacred lake and if there really was an El Dorado, then a remarkable treasure could lie hidden beneath its murky waters. While fortune hunters are lured by gold and precious stones, archeologists are interested in the site for other reasons. Many native objects and writings were lost or destroyed when Europeans ventured into South America. The artifacts in Lake Guatavita could tell much about that period of history, one that has been largely lost in time.

Part III

....

ANALYZING
THE
CLUES

7. EXAMINING ARTIFACTS

The Case of THE LOST KING

In 1976 archeologist Manolis Andronicos began to dig in a promising mound of dirt close to the village of Vergina in northern Greece. In part of the mound, under layers of hardened soil, Andronicos found broken gravestones dating from the fourth or early third century B.C. The gravestones seemed to have been purposely buried, covered ages ago with heaps of dirt to protect and conceal them from looters. Convinced that he had located an ancient Greek burial site, Andronicos arranged to excavate more of the mound the following year.

In the fall of 1977 Andronicos and his crew returned to the site. Over a 35-day period they dug five test trenches through the mound and hauled away 40 000 tonnes of dirt. But they found nothing. No gravestones. No trace of artifacts.

Bitterly disappointed, Andronicos wondered if he had been wrong. He stood wearily on the mound and looked out at the site. He gazed at the piles of earth and stone and at the five trenches carved through the soil. Nothing seemed out of the ordinary.

Then his eye caught something. The soil on the exposed south-western slope seemed different, more compact, a different shade or texture. Could this be another mound, a smaller, older one hidden beneath the larger one?

Andronicos directed his crew to the spot. There was indeed a smaller mound. Inside it, buried just below the surface, they found three tombs. One had been destroyed — only its foundation remained. The other two were intact.

Andronicos entered the smaller tomb first. This tomb had been plundered long ago, but the archeologist still marvelled at the majesty of it. Paintings covered the inside. A man driving a four-horse chariot thundered along one wall; a seated woman gazed out from another.

Massive marble doors guarded the entrance to the second,

larger tomb, which seemed to be intact. To avoid digging out the entire structure Andronicos chose to enter the tomb through its roof. A stone was wedged free and, for the first time in centuries, sunlight streamed into the dark cavern.

Andronicos' own words capture the thrill of the moment: "A little dirt and dust trickled into it, a rectangular black hole. What did the darkness hide? Emptiness — or everything I dared hope for? 'Be calm, as calm as possible,' I told myself. But I think my hands shook a little."

Brandishing a flashlight, Andronicos peered into the tomb. He spotted a marble sarcophagus, its top sealed with a heavy stone slab. Scattered about, he could see the glitter of objects of silver, bronze and gold.

A ladder was lowered through the opening and Andronicos and his workers slipped inside. The sarcophagus was positioned along one wall. Around it were personal belongings — body armour, sandals, a sword, a sceptre, and a diadem or headband. In front of the sarcophagus, fragments of wooden furniture littered the floor. The wood had decayed, but its ivory and gold decorations had survived the passage of time.

Tempting as it was to open the sarcophagus, Andronicos first spent a day measuring, sketching and photographing everything. Finally, on the third day, the stone lid was raised and a surprising discovery made.

The excavators expected to find a funeral urn inside the sarcophagus. Instead they found a larnax, a casket of solid gold. The lid was decorated with a raised sunburst pattern, and the sides were richly engraved. Inside the casket lay charred bones. They had been carefully cleaned and covered with a wreath of oak leaves and acorns.

In a smaller adjoining room or antechamber Andronicos found another sarcophagus. This one too contained a golden casket, with the same sunburst pattern on the lid. Inside were more burned bones. These were wrapped in a purple fabric interwoven with threads of gold. Beside the bones lay a diadem of golden branches and flowers.

Clearly this was no ordinary tomb and these were not the remains of ordinary people. The objects enclosed in the tomb indicated persons of wealth and position. The care afforded the remains signified respect and honour.

Who were the mysterious dead?

No inscriptions or historical record were found at the site to answer this question, but a number of clues were collected.

Clue: Among the artifacts at the tomb were red figure vases dating no later than 320 B.C., and an oil lamp made no earlier than 350 B.C. This pinpointed the burial to some time between 350 and 320 B.C.

Clue: The two caskets were found within a single tomb, suggesting that the dead were related by family or by historical events.

Clue: Both caskets bore the sunburst emblem, a symbol used by the royalty of Macedon, the kingdom that controlled much of Greece in the fourth century B.C. A diadem, the decorative headband worn by kings and queens, was found with each sarcophagus. This evidence suggested that the dead were from the royal house of Macedon.

Clue: Among the bones in the first casket, two teeth were discovered. An analysis revealed that they belonged to a man older than 32 years of age.

Clue: Bronze greaves — leg armour worn below the knees — were also found in the tomb. The greaves were of distinctly unequal lengths and shapes, hinting that the man who once wore them had been wounded in battle and walked with an uneven gait.

So who were the dead? The evidence suggested that the first casket contained the remains of a middle-aged Macedonian king, a warrior who had been wounded in battle, walked with a limp, and died in the late fourth century B.C.

For Andronicos only one historical figure matched the clues. One name echoed from the pages of the past — that of a fearless king, his grave lost in time, his deeds not forgotten.

Philip II of Macedon.

Philip had been a mighty ruler, a natural leader and politician. Under his direction Greece entered a golden age. His 23 year reign sparked changes in architecture, art, philosophy, music and government that affect us even today.

But Philip is remembered more for his conquests. He forged a powerful army and marched from one victory to another. He united the independent states of Greece under his rule, then set his sights on conquering the rest of the world.

Philip paid a heavy price for his triumphs. In one battle he lost an eye; in another he was wounded in the leg, which forced him to walk with a limp for the rest of his life. Then in 336 B.C., at the age of 46, his greatest dream was cut short by tragedy.

With Greece in his control, Philip planned to invade other countries. He organized an army 10 000 strong and prepared to lead it into battle. Only one obligation stood in the way of his departure — the summer wedding of his favourite daughter. While his troops marched ahead, Philip stayed behind to attend the festive occasion.

It was a fatal mistake.

At the wedding feast Philip raised a cup to toast the newlyweds. As he did, an assassin lunged out of the crowd, sword in hand. With a single blow he stabbed Philip through the heart, killing him on the spot.

In the tradition of the times, Philip's body was cremated. The charred bones were collected, placed in a casket and enclosed in a tomb. According to Andronicos' interpretation, the cremated remains of another member of the royal family, possibly Philip's wife Cleopatra, were also entombed, perhaps later. Then dirt was heaped over the site to protect it from intruders, and in time the grave was forgotten.

At first some archeologists were skeptical of Andronicos' idea. The tomb could be the burial site of some other Macedonian nobleman, they claimed.

But Andronicos disagreed. He pointed out that Philip was the only king who died in the right time period and was buried in Macedon. Furthermore, Philip was the only king who had a disfigurement that matched the armour found in the tomb.

But one more discovery links Philip to the forgotten tomb. On his first day inside the tomb Andronicos found five tiny ivory beads on the floor near the sarcophagus. Each bead had been carved into the shape of a small head. At the time he paid little attention to them. But one night more than a week later he took a closer look at one of them.

"I could not believe my eyes," Andronicos later wrote. "It was an excellent portrait of Philip. Here was a mature man with a somewhat fatigued expression, an injured eye, but clearly with great strength of character."

Andronicos recognized the other heads too. They portrayed members of Philip's family — his son Alexander (later known as Alexander the Great), his wife, and his parents.

The tiny heads by themselves do not identify the tomb as Philip's. Neither do the greaves, nor the teeth in the casket. A single artifact or bone cannot provide proof.

But in this case each object adds to the evidence provided by others. The clues match. They support one another, making the conclusion stronger and more convincing.

The evidence points in one direction. This is the tomb of Philip II, lost king of Macedon.

DETECTIVE FILE #7

NOTES: In the Lab

Once objects are removed from the site they are brought to a laboratory for study. Often a temporary lab, a separate tent or trailer, is used at the dig site. Later the objects are moved to a more permanent lab in a museum or university.

To be able to tell the story of the past the archeologist must know where each object came from on the site. All objects are therefore handled carefully. Each artifact taken from one layer and square is kept with other artifacts from the same layer and square.

One of the first tasks in the lab is the initial sorting or

classifying of artifacts. Usually this means grouping them according to the material from which they are made. Objects made of wood compose one group, objects of metal another, and so on.

Then the objects are cleaned and treated to ensure preservation. Pottery and stone artifacts are washed under running water. Waterlogged wooden objects are wrapped in wet newspaper or placed in plastic bags until they can be treated in a permanent lab. This retains moisture and prevents the cracking and splitting that would occur if they dried too quickly. Rust is carefully removed from iron artifacts.

Once objects are cleaned and dried they are brought to a numbering bench to be catalogued. Each artifact is given a code of numbers and letters that identifies the site, square and layer from which it was taken. The code is carefully marked on the object with ink or paint.

Significant artifacts are photographed after they have been cleaned and catalogued. Usually a ruler is included in the picture to show the size of the object at a glance.

Once all the artifacts have been catalogued, objects from different parts of the site can be considered together. Now the archeologist re-sorts the objects, this time looking for patterns or connections between them. Each connection raises questions and leads to hypotheses about the past.

Perhaps several different objects were found close together. Is there some relationship between them? Were they deposited at the same time or in the same way? Could they be part of something larger? Together what do they tell about the society that made them?

Artifacts are often broken. Like an ancient jigsaw puzzle, the fragments must be fitted together. The results can be interesting. Once reassembled, scattered shards of pottery may make a vase; bits of paper, a page from a manuscript; segments of bone, a skeleton. New clues come to light as such connections are established.

Sometimes objects are incomplete, with parts or pieces missing. A skilled technician, artist or scientist may be asked to reconstruct the object from the pieces that are available. By studying the known pieces the specialist can hypothesize about the sizes, shapes and materials of the missing parts.

Using this information, missing pieces may be created out of clay, wood or other materials. The object can then be assembled from original and new pieces together. In this way a complete skull might be reconstructed from a single jawbone, or an entire ship rebuilt from a few preserved timbers.

Computers can be very helpful with the recording, sorting and classifying process. The size, shape and location of each artifact is entered into the computer's memory along with other statistics. By matching these details with those from other artifacts and even other sites, the computer enables the archeologist to compare and classify artifacts and draw inferences about the site more quickly and efficiently.

DETECTIVE CHALLENGE: "Reading" Waste

Jewels, crowns and golden thrones are not always the most important artifacts that lie hidden beneath the soil. Often archeologists learn more about the ways of early people from their garbage than from any other single source.

In 1972 a team of researchers from the University of Arizona conducted an unusual study. They analyzed the garbage pails and wastebaskets of over 600 households in the city of Tucson, Arizona.

The study revealed a lot about the people of Tucson. For example, the researchers found that whether people were young or old, the kinds of materials they discarded were much the same. Middle class groups, however, threw away more food than others. Some households even threw away as much as a hundred dollars worth of unwrapped steak in a single year!

What kind of information can you glean from a wastebasket? Here is a research project you can conduct yourself.

Materials:
- newspaper
- a wastebasket or refuse container from a kitchen, classroom or office

What to Do:
1) Spread the newspaper on the floor or ground outside.
2) Empty the wastebasket onto the newspaper. Spread out the contents.
3) Sort through the "artifacts." Put them into groups or categories — paper products in one pile, food scraps in another, metal cans in a third, plastic objects in a fourth, etc. Use any classification system that suits the materials in the wastebasket.
4) Analyze each group of items. What do they tell about the habits and patterns of the waste producers?

Ask yourself questions:

What kind of diet do these people have? What kinds of foods do they buy? Do they prefer fresh, frozen or canned? Do they throw out a lot of unopened foods? What do these things tell you about them?

Are there any bills? Discarded mail or envelopes? What can you learn from them?

Can you find any discarded reading material? What kinds of publications do these people read? Do they subscribe to a newspaper? What part of the newspaper is most frequently used? What do you learn from these things?

5) If possible, check out your findings with the people who discarded the material. Were your inferences correct?

Digging Deeper:

Try a few other "junk" places. What would the articles in an old trunk or packing case tell you? What could you learn by analyzing the trunk of a car?

DETECTIVE CHALLENGE: Reconstruction

Not all objects unearthed at a dig site are intact. Some are chipped or broken. Others have pieces missing. Before the archeological team can study and interpret the past, such objects may need to to be reconstructed.

Here is a reconstruction activity for you to try.

Materials:
- a cup, saucer or clay pot that you have permission to use for this activity
- a paper or plastic bag
- a hammer
- transparent tape
- ceramic glue or white glue

What to Do:
1) Place your object in the bag. Hit it gently with the hammer to break it into a dozen or more pieces.
2) Shake the bag. This will imitate the disorder an archeologist faces when an artifact is found in a broken state.
3) Try to reconstruct the object. Use pieces of tape to hold the parts in place temporarily. When you are finished, glue the pieces and set the object aside to dry.

Digging Deeper:

Want more challenge? Break another object and throw away a few pieces before you reconstruct it. Or try breaking more than one similar object together. Or have a friend break an object you haven't seen so you have to guess what you are reconstructing. These activities imitate the problems an archeologist faces when artifacts are recovered from a real site.

TIME PROBE: Interpreting Artifacts

On the Trail of the First People

Two hundred thousand years ago the continents of North and South America were without people. Then during the last Ice Age — a period that ended 10 000 years ago — humans arrived in this part of the world.

They came from the west across a narrow northern channel known today as the Bering Strait. During the Ice Age ocean levels were lower, so the floor of the strait was exposed. This natural land bridge enabled people and animals to cross from Asia into present-day Alaska. Later, when the climate warmed once more, the ice melted, water levels rose and the land bridge disappeared.

These early people followed the moving herds that they hunted for food. They lived in temporary camps where they fashioned tools and weapons out of stone and bone. They moved quickly and often, spreading farther east and south.

These were the first people, the ancestors of the native peoples of North and South America. Eventually they covered the two continents, spreading from the northern reaches of Canada to the southern part of the Andes. Over time they separated into many tribes, each one distinct from the others in customs and language.

Archeologists have located many early encampments and studied thousands of artifacts. They have looked at clues and formed hypotheses about the peopling of the Americas. Yet despite a wealth of evidence many scientists do not agree with one another and important questions remain unresolved.

Who were the migrating people? When did they arrive? Why did they come? Why did they scatter and spread as they did?

To understand some of the difficulties facing scientists, imagine that you are part of an archeological team working at one of these early camps. You uncover a long object in the hard-packed dirt — a bone. You carefully pry it loose. The bone is slender, likely the leg bone of some animal, perhaps a caribou. One end is broken, worn to a sharp jagged edge. Fine grooves circle its sides.

After it has been cleaned and catalogued you announce your find to other archeologists. The bone, you suggest, was probably a scraper or flesher, a tool used to remove meat from hides. As proof you point to the sharp edge. It seems obvious that a human hand has shaped the bone into its present form.

Many of your colleagues agree with your interpretation. But one archeologist is skeptical. She has studied the bone carefully using a microscope. She points out that the irregular pattern of the jagged edge and the fine grooves that line it may indicate the tooth marks of another animal. Perhaps this bone was chewed and gnawed by a predator. It might not be the work of man at all, but the work of nature.

Is this bone an artifact — an instrument made and used by humans? Or is it a geofact — an object worn and shaped by natural processes, in this case the gnawing of an animal?

Establishing the authenticity of such artifacts is one of the problems facing archeologists who study early people. Most artifacts from that period are made of stone, bone and antler. These materials survive well over time, but they are also affected by natural forces such as wind, water, erosion and the actions of animals. Distinguishing artifacts from geofacts is not always easy.

Even when an artifact is genuine, the archeologist still has to determine its significance. For example, if a spear point is found near the remains of an animal, does that mean that the two had some connection in the past? The animal may have been killed by the spear. But it is also possible that natural forces —

travelling water or ice perhaps — placed the spear point near unrelated animal remains.

Despite these difficulties scientists continue their search for clues. They gather more evidence, study artifacts in greater detail, separate false leads from true ones. Each artifact is compared with many others, each site with other sites across two continents. Piece by piece, clue by clue, the story of the first people is coming closer to completion.

8. STALKING THE UNSEEN

The Case of THE BODY IN THE BOG

In May of 1950 two men were cutting peat from a bog near
Tollund, a village in Denmark. As their shovels carved away
chunks of peat, a dark brown face suddenly appeared in the soil.
A few more scoops exposed parts of a man's body.

His face seemed so fresh, so alive-looking, that the diggers
thought they had uncovered the body of a recent murder victim.
They wasted no time. Scrambling out of the pit, they ran to call
the police in the nearby town of Silkeborg.

After hearing the details the police were convinced that this
death was not a recent one. They called upon a professor of
European archeology to assist in the investigation of Tollund
man, as the discovery came to be called.

Tollund man lay on his right side near the bottom of the bog,
where he had been covered by two and a half metres of peat.
Because of the depth it was clear that his body had been in the
bog for many years, perhaps even centuries.

The dead man's knees were drawn up, his arms crossed, his
eyes closed as if he was peacefully asleep. Only when a piece of
peat next to his head was removed did the story behind his
death become clearer. Around his neck, twisted and tightly
knotted, was a leather rope. Tollund man hadn't died peacefully
at all. He had been hanged.

Bodies had been discovered in bogs across Europe before.
Some of the victims had been hanged, others drowned. Most had
been placed in the bog after their death. Many of the bodies were
badly decomposed when they were found. But Tollund man was
different. His body was well preserved. It was obvious that
someone had closed his eyes and mouth, then carefully arranged
his body in a sleeping position.

A peat bog often has a history hundreds of years old. Usually
the bog starts as a lake. Mosses called sphagnum or peat moss
grow in the lake. As one generation of moss dies, it sinks in the

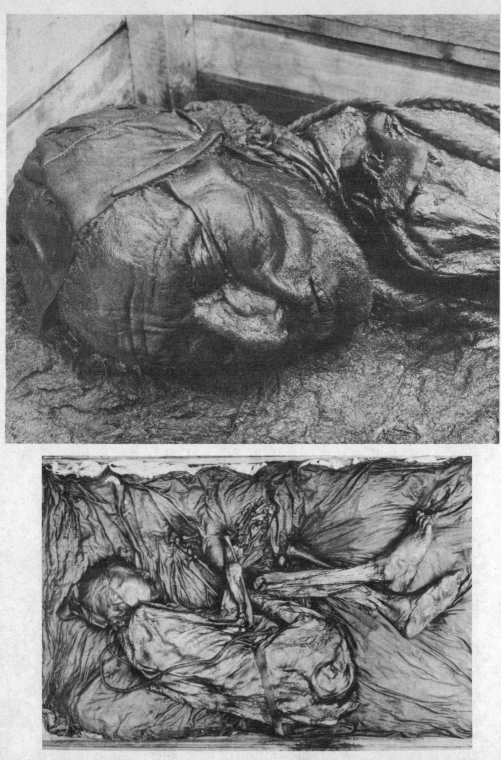

Courtesy of the Danish National Museum

lake and a new one takes its place. Over many years layers of dead moss settle to the bottom. The moss decays, releasing acids into the water. While the top layer of peat is wet and spongy, the weight of the water above packs the lower layers so tightly that water and oxygen cannot pass through. Any organic matter sealed in the lower layers of peat decays very slowly, preserved by the acids in the bog water.

Tollund man's face was particularly well preserved. The acids in the bog had stained it the same brown colour as the surrounding peat. Short stubble covered its surface, but the skin was smooth and taut, the cheeks full, the brow slightly wrinkled. Its expression was one of calm and dignity.

The head was covered with a pointed cap made from eight pieces of sheepskin sewn together and tied on under the chin. Except for a leather belt knotted around the stomach, the rest of the body was naked. The skin hung loosely on the bony frame.

In order to prevent decay and to allow further study, the body and the peat around it were lifted from the pit, crated and shipped to the National Museum in Copenhagen. There the detective work began in earnest. Clearly Tollund man had been killed many years before, but scientists found many of their questions unanswered. Why had he been executed? Who were his murderers? If he had been merely a criminal, then why had his body been so carefully placed in the bog?

The scientific study of the body started with a physical examination. Measurements showed that Tollund man was 173 centimetres tall. He had wisdom teeth, which meant that he must have been more than 20 years old. From all appearances he had been in good health at the time of his death.

To probe deeper scientists conducted an autopsy on the body. Inside the stomach they found hundreds of tiny seeds. Under the high magnification of a microscope, seeds from dozens of kinds of plants, both cultivated and wild, were identified. No trace of meat, nor any leaves or fruit, were found.

The autopsy showed that 12 to 24 hours before his death, Tollund man had eaten a last meal of a type of porridge made from grains, seeds and linseed oil. One of the grains was a form of barley not grown after A.D. 200. Linseed oil, however, was not common in Denmark before 400 B.C. This meant that Tollund man must have died between 400 B.C. and A.D. 200, during a period known as the Iron Age.

To find more clues that would help explain the mysterious death scientists turned to historical records. The Iron Age people had no written language, but they had been invaded by the ancient Romans, who left many detailed accounts of their conquests. One Roman historian, Tacitus, described the habits and rituals of northern tribes.

Tacitus gave two explanations for bog deaths. One concerned punishment. Men and women who committed serious crimes were often hanged or dumped into a bog and weighted down there. The other explanation involved the religion of the Iron Age people.

At that time bogs were thought to be the dwelling places of the gods. Often Iron Age people made offerings to the gods by leaving tributes of meat or porridge in the bogs. Although there were many gods, the main one was Mother Earth, the goddess of fertiliy. According to Tacitus even humans were sometimes sacrificed to Mother Earth to gain her support.

By combining the facts uncovered by scientists, the details provided by Tacitus, and the information known about other bog deaths, a hazy picture of the events surrounding Tollund man's death began to form.

● ● ●

The winter had been long and cold, but now there were signs that Mother Earth was stirring restlessly. The tribe gathered in the sacred grove, a place close to Mother Earth. Here they would give her a gift, a tribute to guarantee that life would once again return to the land.

The gift had to be the best, the finest the people could offer. From among their ranks one man was chosen. He was at the prime of life, at the peak of his fitness. Graciously he accepted the honour. He readied himself for the final event by eating the carefully prepared ceremonial meal, a mixture of seeds, grain and oil. These were the final remnants of the winter food supplies.

At the appointed hour, in a sacred spot near the place which would one day be Tollund, a leather noose was fitted over his neck and pulled tight. In the ancient tradition of the people the man was hanged. Then his body was carefully laid to rest in the bog, the home of Mother Earth.

The air was frosty, the ground firm and cold. But the people were confident. Surely now Mother Earth would return their gift. Surely now the soil would warm, the seeds would sprout, and the glory of Mother Earth would return once again to the land.

● ● ●

While no one can be certain of the exact events behind Tollund man's death, another body discovered a short distance from Tollund two years later supports this view.

Grauballe man, as the second body came to be known, was also discovered by peat cutters. He was around 30 years old when he died. His hands showed that he never had to do much manual labour. From all appearances he too had eaten a ritual meal shortly before his death. The remains of a thick porridge containing at least sixty different types of grains and seeds was found in his stomach. Like Tollund man he had died violently, his throat cut. Was his blood spilled as a further offering to Mother Earth?

After completing their investigations, scientists decided to preserve the two bog bodies. In the case of Tollund man only the head was saved, but the whole of Grauballe man's body was preserved. Using a method similar to the natural tanning process of the bog, Grauballe man was soaked in concentrated chemical solutions for more than a year and a half. Then his body was bathed in oils and impregnated with glycerin, lanolin and collodion.

Today the remains of Tollund man and Grauballe man can both be viewed at the Silkeborg Museum in Denmark, still looking much as they did when they died in the Iron Age over 2 000 years ago.

NOTES: Hunting the Hidden

Tools, weapons, clothing, bones and stones — these are obvious clues to the past. But not all evidence is so large or so obvious.

Very small objects can be revealing too. A single bead from a necklace, for instance, can tell a lot about the customs, trading patterns and resources of the people it belonged to. Tiny seeds can tell what kinds of plants the people grew and harvested. A single fish scale can help pinpoint what species of fish they dined on and even the period in which the fish died.

But sometimes clues are even smaller and less obvious. To detect and study them requires highly developed skills of observation, and sometimes special tools and tests.

One of the most useful tools for small-scale detection is the microscope. With it scientists examine minute cells and particles. Under high power magnification a single human hair can reveal the race, sex and age of its owner. Specks of pollen can help identify the plants that once grew in a region. Tiny, almost invisible scratches on a stone tool can tell how the tool was held and used. The fibres in a scrap of paper can be magnified and identified to tell scientists what materials were used to make the paper and perhaps even the way it was made.

Chemical tests can be useful too. A sample of soil from an archeological layer, for instance, might be tested with chemicals to determine its acidity. Acidic soil tends to indicate the presence of coniferous or needle-bearing trees such as spruce, pine or fir. Less acidic soil may indicate deciduous or leafy trees such as oak, maple or birch. The amount of acid in the soil can thus tell what kinds of plants once grew in the area.

X-rays are also useful to archeologists. Sensitive film is exposed to X-rays that have been passed through an object. The resulting image allows the archeologists to see details inside the object that they couldn't otherwise see. X-rays are used to examine the inside of artifacts and materials that need to be preserved. A wrapped bundle such as a mummy, for example, can be X-rayed without being unwrapped or disturbed, so scientists can learn what is inside the bundle without damaging it.

X-rays can also be used to detect details such as cracks or designs in the surface of vases, jars and other objects. Sometimes they can show what materials were used to make an artifact and how they were applied. An X-ray of a painting, for instance, may show the outline of an older picture beneath more recent layers of paint. X-rays can even help to pinpoint frauds.

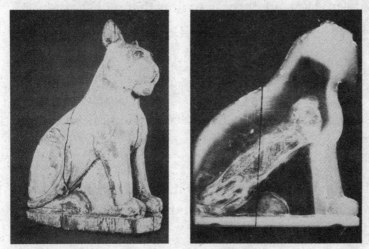

X-ray of a mummified kitten

Royal Infirmary, Manchester Univ., © Dept. of Medical Illustration

Other scientific techniques help archeologists pinpoint the source of artifacts. For example, a beam of ultraviolet light on certain materials will cause them to glow red, blue, green or other colours. Scientists use the colours and degree of brightness to identify the chemicals in the raw material, which may allow them to pinpoint where it came from. Such information helps archeologists understand the trading patterns of ancient people.

DETECTIVE CHALLENGE: Seeing the Unseen

Perhaps you've had this experience:

One day as you are sitting in your room you spot an object on a dresser or shelf. There is nothing unusual about the object — you've looked at it a hundred times before. But now for the first time you see something different — a small crack perhaps, or an unusual colour combination. That's funny, you think, I've never noticed that before . . .

Sometimes we are jarred by unexpected observations and discoveries. Sometimes quite by accident we spot the unusual in the commonplace. Scientists, however, do not rely on accidents. They practise careful and systematic observations, always on the lookout for new clues and insights, even in the ordinary and routine.

With practice you too can refine your ability to see what at first cannot be seen. Here are three activities that will sharpen your skills of observation.

I. A Closer Look

Materials:
- a small object such as a figurine, tool, piece of clothing, or utensil
- paper and pencil

What to Do:
1) Place the object in front of you. Study it for ten seconds, then stop and make a list of all the features you can recall without looking back.
2) Study the object for ten more seconds. Look for small, unnoticed details such as lines, colours and shapes. Stop and add these to your list of features.

How many things were you able to add to your list? What kinds of things did you notice the second time that you missed the first time?
3) Repeat this exercise with other objects. With practice you should notice improvement in the kinds and numbers of observations you make in your first ten-second study of an object.

II. The Ground Beneath Your Feet

What's beneath your feet when you stand outdoors? Most people would say dirt and grass. Those are obvious answers. But the ground beneath your feet holds surprises, many of them not obvious to the casual observer.

This activity is designed to have you look closer, to notice things you may have only taken for granted before.

Materials:
- paper and pencil
- magnifying glass
- Popsicle sticks, tongue depressors or other small sticks
- coat hanger or other piece of wire

What to Do:
1) Make a circle of wire by bending and reshaping the coat hanger.
2) Find a grassy spot outdoors. Throw the wire circle on the ground to mark off a plot of soil for your study.
3) Stand over your plot of soil. Make a list of all the things you notice about it from that height.
4) Kneel or crouch over the plot. Write down all the things you now notice. Include rocks, plants, insects and so forth. Continue with your list until you are confident that you have included everything that can be seen in the plot of soil.
5) Now use the magnifying glass to get a closer look. What kinds of things can you add to your list?
6) Use the small sticks to dig into the soil. Add to your list whatever you find just below the surface. Include rocks, roots, worms, burrowing insects, etc.
7) Pick up a handful of soil. How does it feel — soft, moist, dry, hard, grainy? How does it smell — fresh, stale, mouldy? Add these observations to your list.

There is far more in a plot of soil than just soil and grass. What kinds of things did you find? How did your list change as you looked closer? How did your observations change when you also used your senses of smell and touch?

III. The Observation Game: (an activity for two or more people)

Materials:
- 15 to 20 small objects such as pens, rulers, nails, kitchen utensils, stones, etc. collected by one member of the team
- towel or small blanket
- pencil and paper

What to Do:

1) Have your partner lay out the items on a table and cover them with a towel or small blanket.

2) When all is ready, position yourself in front of the table and remove the cloth.

3) Study the items for 30 seconds, then turn around and write down the names or descriptions of as many objects as you can recall without looking back.

How many items were you able to list? How good were your descriptions? Can you improve your score with more practice?

4) For an added twist, study the objects, turn around, then ask your friend to remove one or two of them. Study the items again. Can you tell what has been taken away?

TIME PROBE: Searching for the Hidden

What Happened to the Mastodons?

Sometimes clues to the past are not obvious or easily noticed. Sometimes the most useful evidence is hidden, unseen or microscopic in size. Recently this kind of evidence has forced scientists to re-examine their ideas about the extinction of the mastodon, a huge Ice Age mammal.

At one time much of the earth was buried under sheets of ice hundreds of metres thick. Then, more than 10 000 years ago, the climate changed. The earth warmed. The ice slowly melted, creating lakes and rivers where none stood before. New land masses appeared; old ones disappeared. Some plants and animals survived the changes. Others, like the mastodon, did not.

The mastodon was a stocky prehistoric relative of the elephant. It lived in many parts of the northern hemisphere, but when the Ice Age ended, so did the mastodon. It became extinct.

What happened to the mastodons? Until recently most scientists agreed on an explanation. The mastodon, they believed, was a forest browser. It ate tender spruce twigs and needles. But as the ice melted, spruce forests dwindled. Unable to find enough food, the mastodon starved and gradually died off.

Recently a mastodon skeleton discovered in Newark, Ohio has forced scientists to reconsider this explanation. The skeleton was found near the new fourteenth hole of a golf course under almost two metres of boggy soil. Near the animal's rib cage a reddish-brown mass was located — the remains of the mastodon's last meal.

Scientists believe that at the time of the Ice Age the Newark golf course was a lush spruce forest. But when the mastodon's intestinal contents were analyzed, not a trace of spruce was found. Instead the mass contained the remains of water lilies, pondweed and grasses.

Scientists also examined the teeth of the mastodon. Plaque, a hard substance that forms on the enamel of teeth, was scraped off. Embedded in the plaque were particles of pollen which were identified as having come from swamp grass, moss and water lilies.

Clearly this mastodon ate aquatic plants, not spruce. Long-held ideas about mastodons do not fit this new evidence. Some scientists have offered another theory to account for the disappearance of the huge beasts. Perhaps, they suggest, mastodons began to rely on pond plants as the climate changed. Then as the land continued to warm, ponds and wetlands started to dry up and disappear too. Forced to cluster around fewer and fewer water holes, mastodons became easy targets for predators.

Were mastodons forest browsers or pond dwellers? Did they die of starvation or because they were prey for early humans and other animals? Was the cause disappearing forests, vanishing wetlands or both?

The discovery of the Newark mastodon and its new, unexpected evidence has left many questions unanswered.

9. STUDYING BODIES AND BONES

The Case of THE MISSING SAILORS

It takes time to solve a mystery. It took more than a century to unravel one of the most puzzling of all tragedies — the disappearance of the Franklin expedition.

In 1845 two ships carrying 129 men set sail from England in search of a passage through the ice-plugged Canadian Arctic. The ships, the *Terror* and the *Erebus*, were specially equipped with steam-driven engines and carried the latest in technical instruments to combat the frigid conditions of the north. Ample food and supplies — enough to last three years and even longer — were loaded on board. Sir John Franklin, an officer experienced in Arctic exploration, was in command.

The expedition had all the earmarks of success. But something went terribly wrong. Franklin, his crew and the two ships never returned to England. They vanished in the frozen Arctic.

For over a decade one search party after another combed the far north seeking signs of the doomed expedition. Aside from three graves, an abandoned lifeboat containing two skeletons, some personal items and a few books and scrawled notes, few clues were found. One hundred and twenty-nine men and two ships had disappeared with hardly a trace.

The British navy examined the scanty evidence and pieced together a story of the expedition's final days. The story matched the clues, but it left many disturbing questions unanswered.

In the summer of 1845 the *Terror* and the *Erebus* sailed through Lancaster Sound north of Baffin Island and the men began to explore. When winter arrived and the two ships became locked in heavy ice, a camp was established on tiny Beechey Island.

During the harsh months of that first winter three sailors died. Their bodies were carefully buried in the frozen ground on the shore of the island.

Spring finally arrived. The ice slowly broke and the two ships were freed. Because the sailing season was short, the expedition could only travel a short distance. Franklin led his men south to King William Island. There they anchored the ships in a channel off its west coast and prepared to wait out a second winter. Death claimed more of the men.

The spring of 1847 was slow to arrive. April passed, then May and June. Still the sea remained choked with ice and the ships could not move. On June 11 Franklin died.

As more weeks crept by, the crew began to lose hope. Summer had almost passed and they were still trapped in the ice. Escape was impossible. They were forced to wait out another winter.

Supplies were becoming dangerously low. Still more of the men died. By April 1848, almost three years after leaving England, only 105 of the original 129 men remained.

In desperation the surviving crew hatched a daring plan of escape. They knew of an inland river somewhere to the south. Unlike the sea around the ship, the river would be free of ice. If they could reach and follow it they might be able to get to safety.

On April 26 the men abandoned the two ships, loading lifeboats with supplies and lowering them onto hastily built wooden sledges. They pulled and pushed the supplies across the ice, but the boats were heavy and the men were weak. Slowly, one by one, the men began to die.

As fewer men remained to haul the bulky boats, articles were tossed aside to lighten the load. Too weak to continue, most of the men died in their tracks, leaving a trail of bodies on the ice. Two sailors found shelter and eventual death in a lifeboat. Some men turned around and tried to return to the safety of the ships. The last 30 or so men continued southward across the ice. A few apparently reached the mainland, but none lived long enough to reach the river they were seeking.

The British navy ruled that there were two causes for the deaths: starvation and scurvy. During the final months of the expedition many of the men starved to death. Earlier deaths were due to scurvy, a disease caused by a lack of vitamin C in the diet. Since the voyage was so lengthy, fresh fruits and vegetables — the main sources of vitamin C — could not be taken along.

Instead foods lacking vitamin C such as tinned soups and meats were served nearly every day.

But there seemed to be gaps in this version of the Franklin story. Even if scurvy was a problem, the number of deaths in the first two winters was higher than expected. And what of the decisions made by Franklin and the crew? Some of them seemed irrational, risky, even foolish and doomed to failure from the start. Something had gone terribly wrong on this expedition, but the details seemed to be lost in the windswept north.

More than a century later a new group of adventurers became interested in the Franklin tragedy. A team of scientists led by Dr. Owen Beattie, an anthropologist from the University of Alberta, probed the Arctic in search of clues to the mystery. Beattie hoped to gather new evidence of the expedition, particularly skeletal remains of the crew. By using the techniques of modern science he hoped to get information about the health, diet and cause of death of the Franklin men from their bones.

In the summers of 1981 and 1982 Beattie led his team of experts to King William Island, the site of most of the deaths. After more than 130 years the lonely island looked untouched, unchanged. Beattie and his men felt a strange kinship with the Franklin men. With a little imagination they could almost see lifeboats being pushed and pulled across the ice by men too weary and weakto walk.

Little physical evidence remained on the island. Only some pieces of clothing, wood, rope and a few other articles scattered the surface to show where so many men had met a tragic end. But at Booth Point, on the island's southern shore, the researchers found a scatter of 31 human bone fragments. These probably represented one member of the ill-fated crew.

The bones yielded some surprising information. A physical examination showed that the crew had indeed suffered from scurvy and starvation. It even suggested that the last survivors may have resorted to cannibalism. But when Beattie returned to Edmonton and sent the bone fragments to a laboratory for routine testing, he learned that they showed something else too

— an extremely high concentration of lead.

Lead in the body acts as a poison, causing illness and eventual death if enough is present. A person suffering from lead poisoning becomes weaker and more tired. Such a person may behave strangely, becoming irritable, unable to work well with others and prone to simple mistakes in judgment.

Most of the food eaten during Franklin's voyage had been preserved in tin cans, a relatively new innovation at the time. The tin itself wouldn't have caused lead poisoning, but the metal solder holding the seams together might have. The solder was ninety percent lead. It could have contaminated the food and, over the long voyage, gradually poisoned the men.

Beattie was excited by this possibility. It might be the key to the mystery. If he could prove that lead had entered the men's bodies during the expedition, it would help to explain the numerous deaths and surprising decisions made by the crew.

But proof was a long way off. The tests on the Booth Point bone fragments told Beattie how much lead had accumulated in that one body over a lifetime. They didn't prove that lead had entered the body during the expedition. Proof that lead poisoning had occurred during the expedition could only come from tests on tissue and hair samples.

Beattie realized that proof for his theory wouldn't be found on King William Island. Only skeletal remains had been found there. But the proof he sought might be farther north in the three frozen graves on Beechey Island.

In the far north the ground just below the surface remains frozen all year round. Although this makes digging difficult, the frozen conditions are ideal for preserving a body. If the Beechey Island bodies had remained encased in ice over the last 138 years, there was a good chance they would be well enough preserved for samples of tissue and hair to be taken.

In August 1984 Beattie and a team of experts flew to the island. On its shores they found the grave sites, each marked by an inscribed grave marker. Beattie had permission to unearth the bodies, take X-rays and tissue samples, perform autopsies, then return the bodies to their graves. To ensure that everything was left in its original state, the graves were carefully staked, mapped, sketched and photographed before the dig began.

Beattie decided to start with the grave of the first man to die on the expedition, John Torrington. Using trowels, pickaxes and shovels, the layers of gravel and permafrost were gradually chipped away. It was hard work and progress was slow. Two full days of digging were needed before the coffin could finally be seen. Even after the lid was lifted off, more hard work remained. The coffin was filled with ice.

For the last stage of the dig, warm water had to be poured over the ice to gradually melt it. At first only a patch of blue could be seen. But as more of the ice melted, a body wrapped in fabric became visible. Finally when all of the fabric was free of ice, the cloth could be pulled back. Beattie and his co-workers held their breath. They were about to meet John Torrington face to face.

Nothing could have prepared them for the sight. They stared into the half-closed eyes of a young man who looked like he had just awoken from a long sleep. Fourteen decades had passed, yet John Torrington looked almost as he had when he died on January 1, 1846.

Torrington's mouth was partly open, giving his face a pouting look. He wore a striped cotton shirt. His arms and legs had been tied in place with strips of cloth. He wore no shoes or boots.

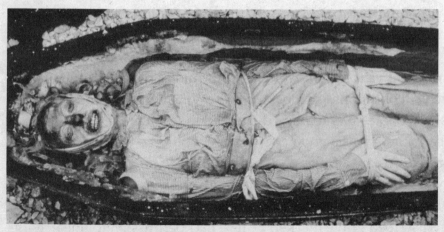

The exhumed body of John Torrington

The body was carefully lifted out of the grave and laid on the ground. A physical examination showed no surface wounds and no obvious signs of illness. A thorough autopsy was done and samples of bone, hair and brain tissue collected. The body was photographed, then carefully placed back in the grave. After a silent prayer was offered, the coffin lid was replaced, gravel was shovelled over it, and Torrington was returned to the arms of time.

Because the season was drawing to a close, Beattie and his team of specialists could not complete their study of the other graves. They gathered a few of the tin cans left behind by the Franklin crew, then left Beechey Island.

In 1986 the team returned to open the two remaining graves, those of John Hartnell, who died on January 4, 1846, and William Braine, who died on April 3, 1846. These bodies too were well preserved. Examinations, X-rays and autopsies were done, and samples collected. Then the bodies were reburied and the site was returned to its original condition.

Would the laboratory tests on the tissue, hair and bone samples prove his theory? Beattie wondered. After weeks of restless waiting, the tests were completed and the results delivered. Nervously he read the report.

All three men had extremely high traces of lead in their bodies even though they had died early in the expedition. The lead had entered their bodies during the few months just before their deaths. It had left them vulnerable to disease, including the pneumonia which actually killed them.

This information made the mystery of the Franklin expedition a little clearer. During the long voyage, lead had leaked into the tinned food. As the crew ate more and more of the food, the levels of lead in their bodies became higher and higher. Over time they were gradually poisoned, left in a weakened state which made them more vulnerable to disease and less able to meet the demands of the voyage and the decisions it required. Lead poisoning, combined with scurvy and starvation, led to tragedy in the frozen Arctic.

NOTES: Bodies and Bones — The Tales They Tell

You've likely heard the phrase "Dead men tell no tales." It's a popular expression. But in the world of modern science it is not true. The dead can tell a lot about the past.

When human remains are uncovered at a dig site a physical anthropologist may be called to investigate them. A physical anthropologist is a scientist who examines, measures and interprets human bodies and bones. From this information the scientist learns about the appearance, habits, health, hardships and triumphs of an individual or a group.

Even a single bone can be revealing. The femur or thigh bone is the longest and strongest bone in the human body. From measurements of this bone alone, the probable height and size of an individual can be calculated.

The study of a skull can reveal an individual's age. When a baby is born its skull is made of several separate bones. As a person ages these bones begin to grow together and eventually become smooth and continuous. By studying how advanced this skull growth is, a person's age at the time of death can be estimated.

Teeth can also help to determine age. Because they grow in over many years and at a set rate — baby teeth, then permanent teeth, then wisdom teeth — an examination of what teeth are present in a skull can be a good indicator of age at death.

Bones can also tell whether an individual is male or female. The skull of a female is normally thinner and lighter than that of a male, while the femur and other bones are shorter. The pelvis or hip bone of a female is wider and shaped differently too.

Bones can tell other stories of the past as well. Worn teeth may indicate great age, but they may also tell about the foods and eating habits of early people. Cracks and fractures may indicate accidents or injuries. Unusual bumps or growth may be signs of illness and disease. Even signs of ancient operations can be detected.

Sometimes a whole population of skeletons can tell a more complete story of the past than a single skeleton. Such is the case in Herculaneum, one of the Italian cities destroyed by the eruption of Vesuvius in A.D. 79.

In 1982 archeologists discovered a large number of skeletons in rooms near what had once been the beach. Apparently many Herculaneans had taken shelter there when the disaster struck. Dr. Sarah Bisel, a physical anthropologist, was asked to study this population of skeletons.

Dr. Bisel was able to read the lives of many individual Herculaneans from their bones. One skeleton has been called Pretty Lady because the shape of her skull shows she had a beautiful face. She also had well-developed arm bones, so Bisel suspects she worked as a weaver. Another skeleton is known as the Soldier. Several missing front teeth and evidence of a serious leg wound suggest that he lived a very rough life. A third skeleton is of a 14-year-old girl who died clutching an infant. Her teeth show that she was starved or very ill as a baby, and her leg and arm bones show that she did a lot of heavy work. She was probably a slave who died trying to protect her owner's baby.

But the group of skeletons as a whole tells a larger story of the Herculanean people of that time. Their average height was shorter than today's, they were generally well nourished, they had good teeth because of their diet, and the slaves among them led very difficult lives. All of this Bisel was able to deduce just from their bones.

Sometimes a well-preserved body, one that includes more than just bones, is unearthed at a site. Because such bodies enable scientists to examine skin, hair and tissues, they provide unique opportunities to understand the past.

Laboratory tests provide many clues. They can reveal information about the age, sex and racial background of an individual. They can also determine the chemical make-up of a body, giving scientists valuable information about diet and diseases of long ago.

An autopsy may also be performed on a body, just as when a person dies today. Autopsies are revealing and can divulge much about the life of an individual. An autopsy on a 2 100-year-old mummy of a Chinese lady, for example, showed that she had gallstones, tuberculosis and a painful back. But none of these caused her death. The arteries leading to her heart were blocked with a build-up of hard material known as plaque. Inside her stomach were 138 melon seeds. Shortly after eating a meal of melon, apparently, she suffered a sudden heart attack and died.

Such autopsies are interesting, but they have drawbacks too. In an autopsy the body is altered and any wrappings may be damaged.

Another way to study a body is to X-ray it. X-rays enable scientists to examine the bone structure and condition of a body without damage. They can be used to establish the age at death, and to show diseases, fractures and other phenomena.

DETECTIVE CHALLENGE: Calculating Body Ratios

Could you predict a person's height from some other body measurement? If you knew the length of a person's arm, for instance, could you calculate that person's height? This is the kind of question that interests a physical anthropologist.

Why not find out for yourself? Conduct a simple research study. Collect data, analyze it and draw your own conclusions.

Materials:
• metre stick or measuring tape
• pencil and paper

What to do:
1) Prepare a chart similar to the one shown below. To be able to draw conclusions, you will need to collect data from at least 5 individuals.

Individual	Height (cm)	Arm length (cm)	Ratio (height/arm length)

2) Measure the height of each person in centimetres.

3) Measure each person's arm length in centimetres. To do this, hold the metre stick under the person's arm and measure the distance from armpit to middle finger.

4) To find the height to arm length ratio, divide the height by the arm length measurement. Is the ratio similar for all people? If it is, you have a handy tool for predicting a person's height.

5) Test your ratio. Measure another person's arm length. Multiply that figure by the ratio. Measure the individual's height and compare it to your calculation. Was your prediction accurate?

Digging Deeper:

What other kinds of body measurements might be used to predict height? Extend your research. Measure head size, leg length, foot length, etc. and compare these figures to height. Do you find other useful ratios? Is it possible to improve the accuracy of your predictions by using more than one measurement for a single person?

TIME PROBE: Human Beginnings

In Search of Our Origins

In many ways the morning of November 30, 1974, was the same as most others for Donald Johanson, a paleoanthropologist. He rose early before the heat of the day, donned his dusty clothes, grabbed his equipment and continued his search for fossils in the desert of the Afar region of Ethiopia, Africa.

But from the start Johanson sensed something different about that day. "When I got up that morning," he later said, "I felt it was one of those days when you should press your luck. One of those days when something terrific might happen."

A few hours later Johanson stumbled upon one of the greatest finds of this century.

Millions of years ago a lake stood on the Afar site. Early human-like creatures called hominids inhabited the grassy plains around the lake. Then over time the lake disappeared. So did the hominids of the region. Only a trail of fossil bones survived to tell their tale.

Who were these hominids of the Afar region? What was their connection to the people of today? These are questions that puzzle scientists like Donald Johanson. Somewhere in the desert soil he hoped to find clues to the past.

That morning as Johanson was leaving an area that had been searched many times before, he spotted something lying on the ground. It was a piece of fossilized bone, part of a hominid arm. Close to it he found the back of a small skull. A short distance away lay part of a femur. Scattered around the site he found even more bits of fossilized bones — some vertebrae (bones of the spine), part of a pelvis, ribs. He was positive that all the bones came from a single individual, a female hominid over three million years old.

Finding hominid bones over three million years old is rare. Finding a number of bones that belong to a single skeleton is nothing short of remarkable. In all Johanson collected hundreds of bone fragments, almost forty percent of a complete skeleton. Never before had such a complete skeleton of one hominid from so long ago been found. Johanson called the hominid Lucy, after a popular Beatles song of the day.

Lucy's bones and teeth told much about her looks and habits. Although she was well over 20 years old at the time of her death, she was tiny — slightly more than a metre tall, little more than 30 kilograms in weight. Her head was the size of a melon. Her slanted forehead, wide brow and flat nose gave her an ape-like look.

But Lucy had human features too. Her jaw and teeth were not ape-like but showed human characteristics in size and shape. More significantly, her pelvis showed that Lucy walked upright on two legs, something apes have never done.

Scientists classify animals into groups based on their physical features and habits. The group known as Primates includes apes, monkeys, lemurs and humans. All primates that stand erect and walk on two legs are known as hominids. Hominids in one form or another have been on earth millions of years. Paleoanthropologists have identified several species of them based on fossil bone specimens.

The hominid species are divided into two groups. One is the genus *Homo*, the group to which humans belong. The other is the genus *Australopithecus*, an earlier, now extinct group. At some point the two groups shared a common ape-like ancestor, but exactly when and how they split apart is unknown.

Where did Lucy fit into this picture? Was she part of the hominid line that later developed into humans? Did she belong to the other hominid group? Or did she come from a time before the two groups separated?

Scientists do not yet agree on the answers to these questions. With the mixed ape and human features shown in her bones it is difficult to tell. Depending on what features of the bones are seen to be most important, the same fossils can lead to very different conclusions.

Some scientists, including Johanson, are convinced that Lucy was not human. They believe that when she was alive there was only one hominid group. Johanson has given her the species name *Australopithecus afarensis*, "southern ape of the Afar plain," and suggested that she and her kind were ancestral to all later hominids, both *Australopithecus* and *Homo*.

But other scientists disagree. They believe that Lucy and others of her kind were more human than not. They place Lucy near the beginning of the separate hominid line that eventually led to our own species, *Homo sapiens*.

Is Lucy a distant human ancestor? Or is she something more removed from us? Many hypotheses are still being investigated. Lucy's place in our human past remains a mystery, one that waits for more evidence and the work of future detectives of time to uncover it.

10. ESTABLISHING TIME

The Case of THE BRITTLE BUNDLES

In the stretch of wilderness between Bethlehem and the Dead Sea in the Middle East the soil is dry and rocky. Except for tribes of wandering nomads known as Bedouins, few people live in this uninviting place. Nevertheless this spot was the scene of one of the greatest archeological adventures of all times.

One day in 1947 a young Bedouin goatherd, Muhammad adh-Dhib, let the animals in his care wander about the craggy hills in search of food. When one of the goats wandered off on its own, Muhammad followed to retrieve it.

High among the rocks he climbed. The sun was blazing in the sky, and Muhammad soon grew hot and tired. He found some shade under an overhanging cliff and sat down to rest. As he gazed around the desert he spotted a small hole about a half metre wide in the cliff face above him.

Idly Muhammad picked up a loose stone, took aim and tossed it into the opening. He was stooping to pick up another stone when he stopped. What was that sound? He had expected to hear the clatter of the stone striking the rock sides of the cave, or perhaps the thud of it hitting the sandy bottom. Instead he had heard a crash as if something had broken. He threw another stone and again heard the smash of something breaking.

Curious now, Muhammad scampered up the rough cliff face, grabbed hold of the jagged rocks around the hole, and pulled himself up. The cave was dimly lit, but as his eyes slowly became accustomed to the darkness he was able to see tall jars, rows of them, standing on the rocky floor. Some of the jars were broken.

Suddenly Muhammad became afraid. No human could inhabit such a place, he thought. Desert spirits must live here. And now he had disturbed their dwelling. Wasting no time, he dropped to the ground and ran off as fast as he could.

Later that evening, at the camp which was his home, Muhammad told the story of his discovery to a friend. The other boy listened closely, his eyes opening wide as Muhammad described the jars. Visions of golden treasure began to dance around in his head. He convinced Muhammad that he had merely imagined the spirits.

The next morning the two friends returned to the cave. They scaled the rocky face, squeezed through the narrow opening, and dropped themselves inside. Exactly as Muhammad had described, rows of jars lined the narrow cave. Some had lids, others didn't. Several jars were empty, but others contained bundles of something so brittle that it crumbled at a touch. Inside one bundle the boys could see a black tarry substance and, below that, smooth brown leather.

Disappointed that they hadn't found gold and jewels, the boys decided to make the best of their find. Perhaps the leather would be worth something and the jars would be useful. They removed some of the objects from the cave and took them back to their camp.

The Bedouins were fascinated by the boys' find. When the elders of the tribe untied the largest bundle and unrolled it across the floor of a tent, they found it was a long scroll covered with strange writing. But they were unable to understand the markings, so they rewrapped the scroll and put it away.

For a time the Bedouins carried the bundles with them as the camp moved from place to place. Then one day when they were in Bethlehem to pick up supplies, they showed the scrolls to a shop owner. He reluctantly agreed to sell them, saying that perhaps the leather might be useful to repair shoes.

Several days later, having reconsidered the scrolls and their strange markings, the store owner took them to Jerusalem where he showed them to a monk at a monastery. Did the monk know what the scrolls said? Were they very old? Could they be worth anything?

The scholarly monk studied the scrolls carefully. The crumbling leather made him believe they must be quite old. They were covered in fine script in a language he recognized as Hebrew. Yes, he decided, the scrolls would undoubtedly be valuable. He gave the storekeeper all he had to purchase these first of what have come to be known as the Dead Sea Scrolls.

According to the law neither of the men should have pursued the matter any further. At the first sign of an archeological discovery they were supposed to report such a find to government officials. But both men realized they had stumbled upon something of value. They made other plans.

The storekeeper located the cave and removed more scrolls. The monk organized his own expedition to the site to look for others. Word of the find spread like wildfire across the desert.

Iris Noble

The scroll of Psalms

Bedouins visited the cave and took everything they thought could be sold. The small cave opening was enlarged. Items that seemed to have no value, such as the broken jars, were tossed in a heap outside.

But the treasure from the cave was no treasure at all until it could be sold. Interested buyers had to be contacted. Phone calls were placed to university professors. Mysterious meetings were arranged. The scrolls were even advertised once in a leading magazine under the heading "Miscellaneous for Sale."

Through such contacts, archeologists were alerted to the discovery. They travelled to the area where the scrolls had been found. From the original cave they excavated scraps of the scrolls' linen wrappings and a few bits of scroll. During the next few years they located other caves containing leather scrolls and scroll fragments, and one cave that contained a large copper scroll.

But a more difficult task was to track down and obtain the scrolls that had been taken by the Bedouin treasure seekers. To increase their profits the Bedouin had broken up the scrolls. They were in thousands of pieces, in dozens of different hands. It took years of hunting and haggling to gather those fragments.

The dry desert air had prevented rotting, but now the pieces were too brittle to handle without further breaking. To treat them, the fragments were dusted off, placed in a humidifier to restore some moisture and make them flexible, then laid between sheets of glass on long tables. Then, like a gigantic jigsaw puzzle, the pieces had to be reassembled. Because the edges were torn and fragments were missing, an exact fit was often impossible. This task took years.

As the fragments were being located and pieced together, scholars began to study the scrolls. They looked genuine, ancient, written in archaic Hebrew, the original language of the Bible. They included passages from almost every book of the Old Testament, as well as other religious writings. The earliest scriptural writings then known were Greek and Latin translations from the fourth century A.D. If these scrolls had been written before that period, they would be the most authentic and complete Biblical passages ever found.

The crucial question was one of time. When had the scrolls been written?

Several methods of dating were used to answer that question. Language experts studied the style of the lettering and the form and meaning of the words. They compared the script on the scrolls to scripts on other writings of known age. Similarly, pottery experts studied the shape and composition of the jars the scrolls had been found in, and compared these to previously dated containers from other sites. Scientists also tested pieces of the linen scroll wrappings using a method known as radiocarbon dating, a process that gives accurate readings of age for objects that are made of plant or animal material.

All of the dating methods gave similar results, each verifying and supporting the others. The Dead Sea Scrolls appeared to date from between the second century B.C. and the first century A.D., which would make them the oldest scriptural writings ever found.

The settlement at Qumran

Iris Noble

But where had the carefully hidden scrolls come from? Where had they been written?

On a plateau known as Qumran near the site of the first cave, the remains of an old Roman camp had long been known. Archeologists looking for the origin of the scrolls found no other likely sites, so they began to dig at Qumran. To their amazement they found evidence of a much larger settlement adjacent to the Roman camp — a settlement that had been burned and completely destroyed.

The settlement had once included cisterns for water, storerooms, kitchen and dining areas, and a long, narrow room furnished with a low table such as ancient scribes would have written on. The discovery of hardened ink in the same room — ink of the same type as used on the scrolls — further suggested that this was where the scrolls had been laboriously copied. A pottery workshop used to make jars like the ones found in the first cave also connected the settlement with the scrolls.

Now the dating of the scrolls could be double-checked. Coins were found throughout the excavation, not many, but of significant dates. The earliest coin dated from 136 B.C., while others ranged up to A.D. 135, the period represented by coins from the Roman camp. The coins confirmed the dates already established. The Dead Sea Scrolls had indeed been written about 2 000 years ago.

But who wrote them? And why had the scrolls been hidden in caves around the Dead Sea?

Some of the scrolls described life in the settlement. Using that information, other ancient writings, and the evidence of the excavation itself, historians have pieced together a likely picture of this little-known society and the strange circumstances that forced it to hide the scrolls.

Almost 200 years before the time of Christ a group of people left Jerusalem to come to the dry, secluded land near the Dead Sea. They wanted to establish a place where they could practise their own religious beliefs without interference.

The centre of activity in Qumran was a large building known as the settlement house. This was where the people of the community ate, worked and practised their religion. Day after day scribes sat or knelt at the long table in one room there. Using quill pens they copied passages of the Old Testament and other writings onto strips of goat and sheep skins. It was most important to these people that the words and messages of these scriptures be recorded accurately for future generations to read.

The community flourished. For 200 years it carried out its work, far away from the activity and turmoil of the outside world. Then in A.D. 68 the life of the people was interrupted. Word reached Qumran that the Jewish people were rebelling against their Roman overlords. In retaliation the powerful Roman army had conquered Jerusalem and was now sweeping into the countryside, determined to crush the people who stood in its way.

The citizens of Qumran knew that it was only a matter of time before the Romans reached their town. Then nothing would be safe. The scrolls had to be saved from destruction. Quickly they set to work gathering the scrolls, wrapping them in linen cloths and placing them in their tall, narrow jars. The jars were sealed and carried into the caves that surrounded Qumran.

The Romans levelled the settlement and scattered its people. A Roman camp was established on the site and remained for many years. But the scrolls stayed safely hidden. For centuries the bundles were protected from decay by the dry desert air. Then finally a stray rock tossed by a Bedouin boy awakened the world to unexpected secrets.

DETECTIVE FILE #10
NOTES: Sleuthing for Time

Imagine that you are an archeologist. As you dig through the layers of dirt in your square, you uncover several objects. Just below the surface you find a tarnished copper coin. Half a metre lower you find a piece of pottery with curious markings. Then a few centimetres deeper you uncover a charred log and a small animal bone.

Many questions puzzle you. How did these objects get here? How were they used? Who used them? Each object has its own story to tell. But each one is part of a bigger, broader story too. Even the four objects together cannot tell that whole tale, since each find in this square relates in some way to finds in other squares and even in other sites.

One of the biggest questions facing you is one of time. If you are to unravel the story of the past, you must establish the order of events, the times and dates when things occurred.

Usually, unless evidence suggests otherwise, archeologists assume that objects found lower in a dig site were deposited earlier than objects found closer to the surface. Of the four objects you uncovered, it's likely that the log and bone came from an earlier time period than the pottery, and that the pottery predates the coin.

But archeologists have other techniques for pinpointing time and dates more exactly. Two main methods are used — relative dating and absolute dating.

Relative dating means that ages or dates are established through comparison with objects of known age or date. To see how this type of dating works, let's use the objects uncovered in your square.

First examine the tarnished coin. Rub it clean. Take a good close look. Do you see a date stamped on it? If you do, you have a helpful dating tool. For instance, if the coin is stamped 1930, you know that it could have been deposited at any time since 1930, but not before then. And because the other objects were found below the coin, they were probably deposited earlier.

The pottery shard provides another clue for relative dating. Decorative fashions used on pottery change over time. Perhaps the curious markings on your shard remind you of those on pottery from another site that has a known age or date. If the newfound piece can be matched to such dated pieces, then it may be possible to assign it a similar age or date.

Absolute dating means that the age of an object is determined through tests on the object itself. The date stamped on your coin is an absolute date. Dendrochronology or tree-ring dating is another method of absolute dating, one that might be used with your charred log.

As a tree grows, new cells are constantly added just inside the bark. In summer these cells are large and light in colour. During winter the cells are small and close together. The contrasting layers of light and dark cells are called growth rings. The size of the growth rings varies according to the weather, creating patterns that are the same in all trees in a region.

Dendrochronologists have made charts of these growth ring patterns going back many years for trees in many different areas. By studying the rings on your log and matching their pattern with an established ring chart, the date your log was cut down may be determined.

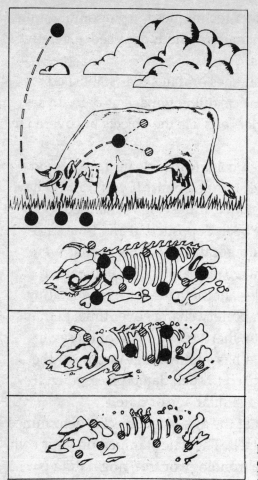

carbon 14 ●

carbon 12 ◑

Carbon 14 enters living things and breaks down into carbon 12 at a balanced rate.

An animal dies and stops taking in new carbon 14, but the carbon 14 present in its body continues to break down.

5,730 years after the animal's death only half of the carbon 14 remains.

Every 5,730 years the amount of carbon 14 is halved, until little or none remains.

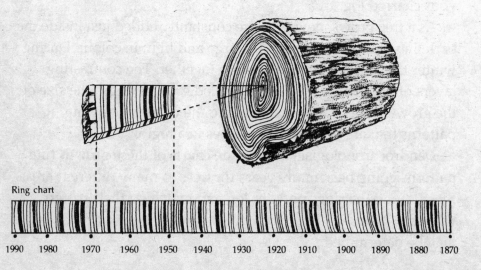

Ring chart

1990   1980   1970   1960   1950   1940   1930   1920   1910   1900   1890   1880   1870

Another form of absolute dating, radiocarbon dating, might be used on either the log or the small animal bone. All living things contain carbon atoms. One form of carbon, carbon 14, is radioactive. That means that particles of such carbon atoms keep breaking off, changing carbon 14 into another type of carbon called carbon 12.

Every living thing, plant or animal, contains both carbon 14 and carbon 12. Carbon 14 continuously breaks down, making more carbon 12. But as long as a plant or animal is alive, new supplies of carbon 14 are constantly taken in, so the ratio of carbon 14 atoms to carbon 12 atoms remains the same.

When the plant or animal dies, however, the situation changes. It stops taking in new supplies of carbon 14, but the carbon 14 already in its tissues continues to break down. Thus the ratio of carbon 14 to carbon 12 starts to change. This change continues at a fixed and steady rate for a very long time.

By measuring the amount of carbon 14 still present in a once-living thing and comparing it to the amount in living tissue, scientists can calculate how long ago a plant or animal died. Such carbon 14 dating can establish fairly accurate dates as far back as 50 000 years.

Another way to establish dates is through thermoluminescence dating or TL dating for short. This method is useful for dating pottery or other artifacts made of fired clay. Clay contains small quantities of radioactive matter. This matter gives off energy, which is stored in the clay. When clay objects are fired in a kiln the high temperature releases the energy. Then over time energy builds up in the object again. By determining the amount of energy released as light when a clay artifact is reheated in the lab, scientists can pinpoint the date that the clay was first fired. Unlike other dating methods, TL dating is accurate for both ancient artifacts and more modern ones.

DETECTIVE CHALLENGE: Pinpointing Dates

How good are you at tracking down dates and times? Here are ten everyday items. Each one is datable in some way. Can you figure out the age of each object or the date it was made? Where would you look for proof? What sources would you consult?

ITEMS:

1. An envelope that has been through the mail
2. A page from a newspaper
3. A five dollar bill
4. An original oil painting
5. A telephone bill
6. A woman's dress
7. A photograph
8. A porcelain figurine
9. A book
10. Your public library

ANSWERS:

1. Check the cancellation date that was stamped on the envelope by the post office. If that does not help, check a stamp catalogue to find out when the stamp was issued.
2. The date is at the top of each page of a newspaper.
3. The year that the money was issued will be stamped on one side of the bill.
4. Original paintings are usually signed by the artist. Sometimes the date is also included. Or you may be able to find the artist's name and painting in a book about art collecting.
5. Utility bills usually have dates printed somewhere on them.
6. Fashion trends change with time. For example, polyester bell-bottom pants, miniskirts, and wild plaids and stripes were in fashion in the 1960s and early 1970s. By the late 1970s these styles had been replaced by others. By studying the style and design of clothing, as well as the fabric from which it is made, you may be able to establish the time period during which it was worn. Consult reference books on fashion trends for further clues.

7. Some photographs have the processing date stamped on the front or back. Look for clues in the photograph too. Styles of dress or background objects might help you estimate the date.

8. Most pieces of pottery and porcelain have a manufacturer's stamp on the bottom. Some manufacturers publish their own catalogues, and these may help establish the date the object was made. Reference books in the public library, such as the *Encyclopedia of Pottery and Porcelain*, can also be useful in tracking down dates.

9. Most books have copyright dates printed on a page near the front.

10. Public buildings such as government offices, schools and libraries often have a cornerstone or plaque that gives the date the building was opened. The land titles office in your city or town also keeps a record of all land and building transactions.

DETECTIVE CHALLENGE: Reading Layers

Try your hand at dating and interpreting layers or strata.

Materials:
- empty wastebasket or garbage can
- masking tape
- tape measure or ruler
- paper and pencil

What to Do:

1) Obtain permission to leave a wastebasket in a classroom, office or other place where people throw away paper. Tell your subjects that you will be analyzing their paper waste and will report your findings to them if they wish.

2) Ask your subjects to throw all of their paper garbage into the wastebasket for a full week. Instruct them to stomp down on the trash to make more room if the wastebasket becomes full. For added interest ask your subjects to occasionally drop in a dated memo, envelope or bill.

3) At the end of the week pick up the wastebasket and begin your study. Place a piece of masking tape on the inside of the wastebasket to mark the location of the topmost layer. Slowly peel back the trash and set it in a pile on the floor. Try to find out where the last day's trash ends and the previous day's trash begins. Use dated letters, bills, envelopes and memos as clues, as well as anything you know about daily activity in that place. Mark the end of the first day's trash on the side of the wastebasket with another piece of masking tape.

4) Continue peeling back the trash and separating it into piles according to the day it was deposited. On the side of the wastebasket, use masking tape to mark each change in layer.

5) When you have excavated the entire wastebasket, measure the depth of each layer. This will be the distance between the strips of masking tape on the side of the wastebasket. Record the figures on a chart similar to the one below. Also list the kinds of waste deposited each day.

Day/Date	Depth of Waste	Kinds of waste

6) Analyze your findings and make inferences. What do you learn about the waste habits of your subjects? Were the same kinds of things thrown out every day? Can you tell on which day(s) most waste was deposited, or why more was tossed away then than on other days? Can you identify who threw away particular items, or why?

Prepare a brief report to give to your subjects. Can you recommend ways they could reduce their waste?

TIME PROBE: Conflicting Evidence

Glozel: Real or Fake?

Is it genuine or a hoax?

That's the question often asked when an artifact turns up in suspicious circumstances. Sometimes establishing dates helps tell original artifacts from forgeries.

In 1924 a young man stumbled upon the remains of a medieval furnace near the town of Glozel in France. As area residents excavated the site they uncovered some unusual articles — prehistoric-like bone tools, clay tablets covered with ancient script, strangely decorated pottery fragments.

For many years archeologists debated whether the objects were genuine or not. Some thought they were carefully crafted forgeries, the work of a clever prankster. Others believed that they were ancient artifacts dating from a thousand years or more before Christ.

In 1974 a team of scientists used TL dating on some of the objects. The results were both surprising and disturbing. The tests established dates of between 700 B.C. and A.D. 100. The objects, therefore, were neither as modern as some argued nor as ancient as others believed.

The explanation? More investigations are still being done on the Glozel articles, but one theory has been suggested. Perhaps the objects were made in modern times, but from ancient materials. A recent forger using ancient bone and clay could have carved or decorated them to resemble genuine artifacts.

At present the Glozel objects remain an archeological mystery.

Part IV

···

INTERPRETING
THE
EVIDENCE

11. DECIPHERING MESSAGES

THE CASE OF THE MYSTERIOUS CODE

Curious writings thousands of years old mark statues, monuments, pyramids and temples in Egypt. These symbols and pictures are called hieroglyophics.

Like words on a page, hieroglyphics are a record of the past. They tell of the births, deaths, triumphs and losses of ancient Egypt.

Until the nineteenth century the hieroglyphics of Egypt remained a mystery. No one, not even Egyptians themselves, knew how to interpret the symbols. The art of reading hieroglyphics had been lost and forgotten over time.

In the summer of 1799 a chance discovery changed the course of history. French soldiers who were demolishing the ruins of an old fort near the town of Rosetta, Egypt, unearthed a strange black stone. The stone was flat, irregularly shaped, the size of a tabletop. Carved into its surface were three sets of markings. Each appeared to be in a different language.

The officer in charge of the expedition, recognizing that the stone might be important, bundled it up and shipped it to Cairo, the capital of Egypt. There it joined other artifacts collected by Napoleon and the French army during their invasion of Egypt. But when Napoleon's army was defeated by the British, the collection was seized by them. The Rosetta Stone, as the artifact became known, was sent to the British Museum in London.

Scholars were able to identify the three sets of markings on the stone. One was in ancient hieroglyphics. Another was in a more modern version of hieroglyphic writing called the demotic script. The third set was written in old Greek.

The Rosetta Stone caused a stir in archeological circles. If, as seemed likely, all three scripts told of the same event, it might be possible to use the Greek text to translate the hieroglyphics. Then perhaps other hieroglyphic messages could also be decoded. The Rosetta Stone promised to be the long-awaited key to Egypt's past.

Rosetta Stone

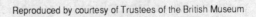

Translating the Greek message was simple enough. The inscription described special honours that had been awarded to King Ptolemy V Epiphanes by the priests of Egypt almost two hundred years before Christ.

But decoding the other symbols was not so easy. Language experts tried many approaches. Some believed that each character or glyph in the message stood for a word. Others believed that each symbol stood for a thought or expression. But all attempts to decode the hieroglyphic writings ended in failure.

Plaster casts of the Rosetta Stone were distributed throughout Europe in the hope that someone would be able to decipher the message. In 1809 Jean-François Champollion, a young Frenchman, first tried his hand at the stone.

From the start Champollion seemed strangely suited to the task, as though fate had been grooming him for the job. As a youngster he had been shown a stone tablet engraved with hieroglyphics and told that no one could read the symbols. Almost as if he could see into the future, the young lad had confidently announced, "I am going to do it."

Champollion was a brilliant scholar. At the age of 5 he taught himself to read. By the time he was 11 he had mastered Hebrew, Latin and Greek, the primary languages of history. At age 13 he began to learn Arabic, Syrian and Caldean, the ancient tongues of the east. Then on his own he started to master Coptic, a language directly descended from early Egyptian. To become fluent in Coptic he practised it daily, often talking to himself in that tongue or using it to write in his diary. At the age of 19 he was made a full professor at the University of Grenoble, the first time anyone so young had been given that honour.

Like scholars before him, at first Champollion assumed each glyph on the Rosetta Stone represented a word. But when he counted the number of symbols on the stone he found that there were three times as many glyphs as there were words in the Greek text. Clearly one glyph did not equal one word.

Champollion decided on a different approach. Perhaps each symbol stood for a sound. That would explain why there were so many glyphs. But what sounds did they represent?

Some of the glyphs on the Rosetta Stone were enclosed in oval boxes or cartouches. Scholars had already determined that the cartouches highlighted royal names. This was the way Egyptian scribes showed honour and distinction to the members of the royal family.

Champollion used this information as his starting point. On the Rosetta Stone there was only one basic cartouche repeated several times. Since the Greek text frequently mentioned Ptolemy, the Egyptian ruler, Champollion assumed that each cartouche enclosed that king's name. Using this clue he began linking the symbols in the cartouche with their Greek equivalents.

The basic cartouche that represented Ptolemy's name looked like this:

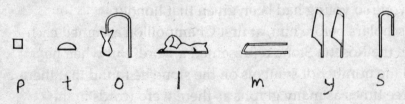

Earlier scholars had tried to decode the glyphs using the Greek translation of the pharaoh's name, *Ptolemaios*. But with his knowledge of Coptic, Champollion realized that it was the proper Egyptian form of the name, *Ptolmys*, that should be used. In this way he was able to give each symbol a logical phonetic or sound value:

The next step came when Champollion was able to study another bilingual inscription, the Philae obelisk. On it he found the name Cleopatra mentioned in the Greek text, with a corresponding cartouche in the hieroglyphic writing:

Champollion noticed that some of the symbols in the Cleopatra cartouche were the same as those found in the Ptolemy cartouche on the Rosetta Stone. Using this link he was able to match up more hieroglyphic symbols to phonetic sounds:

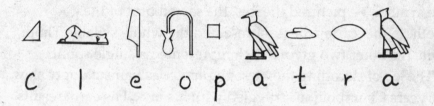

The two identical symbols in the new cartouche must represent the two *a* sounds in Cleopatra. Two of the other symbols matched logically with other sounds. The ⌒ symbol, Champollion decided, must be equivalent to the ⌒ symbol in Ptolemy's cartouche. Both represented the *t* sound, in much the same way that different spellings represent one sound in English (eg. puff, enough). That left only the two final glyphs in the cartouche, which other scholars had already suggested were used to mark a feminine name.

In this way, symbol by symbol, sound by sound, Champollion began to translate the puzzling hieroglyphics. He compiled a list of sound/symbol equivalents and used it to decipher other texts and inscriptions. When he encountered new and unfamiliar glyphs he applied what he already knew of Coptic and hieroglyphics to decode them. His list of sound/symbol equivalents grew with each new success.

But the simple sound/symbol correlation did not always work. Champollion discovered that some hieroglyphic symbols represented not single sounds, but combinations of sounds. The cartouche of the pharaoh Thothmes, for example, contained only three glyphs:

The symbol ⟋⟍ pictured the ibis, the sacred bird of the god Thoth. In this cartouche it represented the whole syllable Thoth, while the other two glyphs each represented a single sound.

The job of decoding the hieroglyphics was painstakingly slow. For years Champollion struggled with his task. His early results were made public in 1822 and 1824, but he continued to work with the hieroglyphics right up until his death in 1832 at the age of 42.

Despite his achievements many of Champollion's colleagues scoffed at his work. Some of his ideas were criticized and ridiculed. Even after his death the debate continued to rage.

Finally in 1866 the controversy ended when scholars translated another bilingual inscription, the Decree of Canopus, using Champollion's decoding system. After that, many hieroglyphic texts were deciphered in the same way. With each new translation the world learned more of the secrets of ancient Egypt. The true genius of Jean-François Champollion was finally recognized.

Today the Rosetta Stone remains on display in the British Museum in London. It is a silent reminder of Egypt's past glory, as well as a striking tribute to the brilliance of Jean-François Champollion.

NOTES: Inscriptions and Codes

Inscriptions etched on pottery, clay tablets, statues and buildings are valuable clues to the language and habits of people from the past.

Reading and understanding strange symbols and alphabets is a difficult job, especially when the language used is no longer written or spoken. Specialists known as epigraphists are often called to translate ancient inscriptions.

Like a detective cracking a spy code, the epigraphist looks for clues in a message. For example, symbols that are repeated often may represent vowel sounds or commonly used sounds such as s, t or h. Small groups of symbols may mean frequently used words such as "of," "is" or "at." A message written in two or three different languages lets the epigraphist compare elements and pick out other clues.

To speed up research by allowing many scholars to work at once, and to ensure that the original artifact remains undamaged, inscriptions are often copied or duplicated. Markings on paper or parchment can be photographed or copied by hand. Engravings in metal or stone must be copied in three dimensions.

One method of copying engravings uses rubber latex. Several coats of latex are brushed onto the engraved surface. After it dries the latex can be peeled off in a soft sheet that bears a mirror image of the inscription. This method is useful for copying large inscriptions.

Ordinary aluminum foil, the kind that can be purchased in a supermarket, can also be used to copy an engraving. The foil is pressed onto the engraved surface and smoothed into place with the fingers. A stiff brush is lightly beaten against it to force it tightly into the inscription. When the foil is then lifted off, a mirror image of the inscription is left on its surface. To produce a right side up image of the inscription a plaster cast must be made. Plaster of Paris is poured in shallow layers onto the foil. When the plaster is hard and dry, the foil is peeled away. A perfect replica of the original inscription can be made this way.

Rubbings can also be used to copy some engravings. To do this, paper is laid over the inscription or etching and charcoal or pencil rubbed lightly across the surface. This transfers a copy of the picture or message directly onto the paper.

DETECTIVE CHALLENGE: Decipher a Message

Suppose you've just unearthed the tomb of a queen. A smooth stone carved with symbols and marks has been found near its entrance. The marks resemble letters from the alphabet, but the letters seem jumbled and mixed:

KHUH OLHV <u>TXHHQ VRUSKDOLXP</u>, D JUHDW DQG ZLVH UXOHU.

    QUEEN SORPHALIUM

GXULQJ KHU UHLJQ KHU FRXQWUB SURVSHUHG DQG KHU SHRSOH ZHUH KDSSB. PDB VKH ILQG SHDFH LQ WKH ZRUOG EHBRQG.

The message makes no sense because it has been written in code. Each letter in the message must stand for another letter in the alphabet.

Fortunately the queen's name has been also been inscribed in its English translation. Knowing the letters used in the queen's name can help you figure out the coded words. Each word that you decode leads you one step closer to deciphering the message.

Here is an alphabet grid to help with the task. Each time you decode a letter in the message, write it in its corresponding place in the grid. Then use the grid to decode other words in the message.

The letters for the word "queen" have been placed in the grid to start you off.

Code	A B C D E F G	H	I J K L M N O P	Q	R S	T U V W	X	Y Z
Normal Alphabet		E		N		Q	U	

Can you decipher the ancient message? Can you crack the code that was used to write it? Is there a pattern to the code?

ANSWERS:

Coded Message:

Here lies Queen Sorphalium, a great and wise ruler. During her reign her country prospered and her people were happy. May she find peace in the world beyond.

Alphabet Grid:

Code   A B C D E F G H I J K L M N O P Q R S T U V W X Y Z

Normal
alphabet X Y Z A B C D E F G H I J K L M N O P Q R S T U V W

Pattern:

The normal alphabet is three spaces to the right of the code alphabet.

Digging Deeper:

Try your hand at making up your own coded messages. Construct an alphabet grid, then write out a message in code. Pass it on to others and see if they can decipher your message.

TIME PROBE: Mysterious Message
The Yarmouth Stone: What Does it Say?

In 1812 a physician named Richard Fletcher stumbled across an unusual boulder in a cove near Yarmouth harbour in Yarmouth, Nova Scotia. Etched across a flat side of the boulder were fourteen marks. They appeared to be letters in a foreign or ancient alphabet.

Since its discovery many experts have examined the Yarmouth Stone. Some maintain that the marks are merely the result of erosion, the work of tides and ocean waves. Others believe that the etchings are the work of a prankster, someone intent on challenging scientists.

Many experts, however, believe that the strange marks are an ancient message, one that was inscribed on the boulder before the time of Columbus. So far the inscription has baffled translators and interpreters. Is the message in Japanese characters, Indian picture writing, ancient Viking symbols or Mycenean letters? All of these, as well as other languages, have been suggested at one time or another.

To date no one has been able to decipher the strange message, or to show conclusive evidence that the marks are the work of either nature or a prankster. The Yarmouth Stone remains as mysterious today as it was when it was first discovered almost two centuries ago.

Nova Scotia Information Service

12. VERIFYING IDEAS

The Case of THE MYSTERIOUS PAINTINGS

The afternoon started as an ordinary venture into a forest for four boys. It ended with one of the most spectacular discoveries ever made in Europe.

On the afternoon of September 12, 1940, the boys set out to do some rabbit hunting in an oak forest near their village of Montignac in southwestern France. They took along a small dog, a fox terrier named Robot. Robot loved to romp through the woods. He never wandered far away and always returned when called.

On this particular day Robot bounded ahead, then unexpectedly disappeared. The boys whistled and called, but Robot did not return. The boys searched the area where they had last seen him, a ridge covered with pine trees called the Lascaux hill. Finally they found a small hole in the hillside just under a short shrub. Listening closely, they could hear muffled barks coming from the opening. Robot had fallen into the hole.

The oldest boy, 17-year-old Marcel Ravidat, quickly took charge. Using his knife he carved away the roots of the shrub, then removed some of the stones. Painstakingly he enlarged the opening until it was wide enough to squeeze through. Then he tossed down some stones and listened. The echoing sounds told him that the interior was large and hollow. The bottom of the cavern was far away, he feared.

Marcel was a cautious boy. He felt responsible for the safety of his friends, so he insisted that they return to the village for rope and light before entering the cave. Then, warning the other boys to wait until he called for them, he crept into the opening headfirst.

By shuffling on his elbows and pushing with his knees, Marcel was able to edge along the narrow shaft. But suddenly he slipped on some loose clay. Down he slid, scraping and bouncing, until he landed on the rocky bottom metres below.

Stiff and sore, he got to his feet. There was plenty of room to stand now. He shone his light up towards the entering passageway high above. Despite the slippery slope the others should be able to manage, he decided. One by one his friends carefully crept and slithered down to the rocky bottom.

Now where was Robot? The boys called and whistled, the sounds bouncing eerily off the walls and ceiling of the cave. Suddenly they heard a clear, sharp bark. In no time Robot was at their feet, leaping and yelping wildly.

With Robot safe, the boys turned to exploring the cave. Marcel led the way, shining his lamp on the jagged walls and ceiling. In the flickering light shadows loomed everywhere and patches of colour spotted the cave. Then suddenly the boys stopped, too stunned to move or speak.

There in full view was the image of a horse galloping across the rocky wall. Behind it raced other horses, their manes flying, their hooves pounding. As Marcel slowly scanned the cave with the light, the boys now recognized other animals too — deer, antelope, bison, bulls. Excitedly they began to wander through the cavern. Everywhere they spotted drawings and paintings.

Prof. Dr. Eric Pietsch

The boys were wild with joy. The cave was their treasure, their own secret. They made a pact. They would not say anything about their discovery, but would return and continue their exploration as soon as possible. Then, using loose stones, they built makeshift stairs and climbed up out of the wonderful cavern.

The next day the four boys left home one by one at ten minute intervals, each taking a different route. This time they were able to explore more of the cave. Using ropes they lowered themselves into deep passages and crevices. They found many more paintings scattered on the walls and ceiling of the cave. Some of them were of single animals; others showed whole herds.

Gradually over the next few days the boys began to realize the importance of their discovery. Clearly these were very old paintings, completed perhaps thousands of years before. Despite their desire to keep the secret to themselves, the boys knew the paintings did not belong to them. Finally, five days after first stumbling upon the cave, they told a teacher of their find. He in turn convinced an archeologist, Abbé Henri Breuil, to visit the site.

When Abbé Breuil reached the cave the boys escorted him through, showing him first one painting, then another. The archeologist examined the pictures in silence. At last he sat on a stone in the cave and motioned for the boys to join him.

"There have been many caves discovered in Europe," he began. "But this cave . . . this treasure as you call it . . . is the most beautiful of them all."

Abbé Breuil did not doubt that the paintings were the work of prehistoric man. Tests have since shown that they were done 15 000 to 20 000 years ago. Because the cave was sealed from outside air for so long, the colours remained as vibrant as the day they were put on the cave walls.

But what was the meaning of the paintings? Were they just decorations made to pass the time? Were they works of art done by a specially chosen artist? Or was there some deeper meaning to them?

For many years experts argued about the meaning and importance of the paintings at Lascaux and other caves. Some animals were drawn in groups or clusters, each group depicting a scene. Others were placed more randomly, even one on top of another. Many appear to be in motion, as if escaping from an enemy. Some figures have arrows and spears drawn in their sides. In one scene a human-like shape is seen throwing a spear at a group of fleeing animals.

From the motion of the animals, their size and colour, and their positions throughout the caves, many experts believe that these paintings had some deep meaning for early man. Perhaps they were part of some ritual or ceremony that was performed before a hunt.

Even today primitive tribal groups are known to hold such ceremonies. Using dancing and song, they try to encourage the success of tomorrow's hunt through ritual magic. They act out a successful hunt, hoping that when the real hunt takes place it will end just as successfully.

Support for the idea that early man conducted similar ceremonies inside caves came to light almost 40 years after the four boys stumbled upon the paintings at Lascaux. Archeologists working in another painted cave, this one in northern Spain, found man-made columns of earth on the cave floor. The columns were arranged in a circular pattern and were carefully made from different colours of clay. Underneath the columns the archeologists found broken bones and burnt plant remains. Nearby they discovered a carved stone face. Half the face was human; the other half was of a large cat, probably a lion or leopard.

This discovery seems to confirm that ritual ceremonies were performed in caves. And since the walls of this cave were painted like so many others, it seems likely that the paintings were part of the mysterious ritual.

With a little imagination it is possible to recreate a scene in such a cave as it might have happened 20 000 years ago.

• • •

Days had passed since the people had any fresh meat. Only a few scraps and bones remained from the last kill. Now they were hungry.

Carefully the hunters prepared their weapons. For hours stones were patiently rubbed against other stones until blunt edges were changed to sharp ones. Then, using strips of hide, the points of stone were tied to sticks to form spears and arrows. At last the hunters were ready.

Before going out to meet the danger of the hunt the men gathered deep in the sacred cave. Offerings were burnt in a small fire in front of the paintings. The voices of the hunters joined in chants, echoing in the dark cavern. Then there was silence.

Each hunter stared at the figures on the cave wall. He imagined his target in front of him. He could sense the animal's power, feel its moist breath, smell its fur, so real did the image seem. The hunter imagined himself stalking the animal. In his mind he saw the animal move. His body tensed. Then raising his weapon, the hunter took careful aim at the image on the wall.

There was magic in the ritual. By rehearsing the hunt, by feeling one with the animal, the hunter knew that he was ensuring a good outcome. Finally he was ready for the real thing.

● ● ●

No one can be sure of the details of these events. But we do know that cave paintings were important to early man for many years. The walls of caves were used and reused repeatedly as people struggled to succeed in an uncertain world.

Whatever their original purpose, the paintings at Lascaux today provide us with a beautiful and haunting record of a time long forgotten.

DETECTIVE FILE #12
NOTES: Experimental Archeology

The archeologist continually examines evidence and makes hypotheses. Eventually, when all the evidence has been weighed, inferences may be drawn to propose explanations for past events.

But are the inferences correct? Are the explanations possible?

One method of checking hypotheses and explanations is through experimental archeology. By using carefully designed experiments, archeologists can test ideas and explanations to see if they are likely or even possible. Sometimes an experiment confirms an idea. Other times an experiment disproves an explanation, forcing it to be discarded or changed in the light of new evidence. Occasionally an experiment opens doors to the past by providing new information never considered before.

One of the most famous archeological experiments of this century was the daring voyage of the *Kon-Tiki* in 1947. For many years scholars wondered how the Polynesian islands of the Pacific became inhabited. Where did the native islanders come from? How did they get to the islands?

The *Kon-Tiki*

A few scholars thought that the islands were peopled by natives from South America who travelled across the Pacific by boat. But most experts rejected that idea. They believed that the boats used by South American natives were too weak and flimsy for such travel.

One anthropologist, Thor Heyerdahl, decided to put the South American boat theory to a test. Using a specially constructed balsa-wood raft similar to the ones used by early South American natives, Heyerdahl and his crew sailed west from South America. Three months later they landed the raft, the *Kon-Tiki*, safely on the Pacific island of Tuamotu.

Heyerdahl's experiment did not prove that the Polynesian islands were colonized by South American natives. But it did show that such a voyage was possible.

Years later Heyerdahl made another voyage, this time across the Atlantic in a papyrus reed boat, the *Ra*. His point? To show that the early people of the Mediterranean could have sailed to Central and South America long before the time of Columbus.

Not all archeological experiments are as dramatic as Heyerdahl's voyages. Many experiments are planned and conducted in laboratories. Such experiments serve many purposes, from testing how tools and weapons were made and used to investigating how ancient people stored and prepared food.

A modern variation of the archeological experiment uses the computer to test ideas and theories. Recently, for example, scientists investigated the Biblical story of Moses and the parting of the Red Sea. In the story Moses led the escaping Hebrews to freedom from Egypt by parting the waters of the Red Sea, thereby providing a land bridge for their passage. Could natural forces such as wind and weather have pushed the waters of the Red Sea aside?

A computer was used to correlate data about location, wind speed, depth of water and other factors. According to the computer calculations the Red Sea was too wide and too deep to have been influenced in this way by natural forces. Nature cannot be used to explain the Bible story.

Whether on site, in a lab or by computer, experimental archeology can add to our understanding of past events.

DETECTIVE CHALLENGE:
Doing an Archeological Experiment

How did early people like those who used the Lascaux cave make dyes and paints? To find out you can do an archeological experiment of your own.

Scientists know that ancient people used the natural materials around them as sources of colour. Berries, leaves, flowers, cones, bark, soil and sand — all of these provided distinctive tones and hues. To release their colours the materials were first chopped and ground, then heated with water or other liquids. Sometimes other ingredients were added to brighten the colours, to make them thicker, or to ensure that they would not fade when applied to fabrics or other surfaces.

Knowing this, you can do an experiment to determine how people made and used colours thousands of years ago.

Materials:

- a pot or other metal container for boiling
- a variety of natural dye sources: roots, berries, leaves, bark, flowers, cones and husks. Some dye sources such as beets, red cabbage, berries and nuts can be purchased from the supermarket. Others must be found in the wild, in the garden or forest
- alum and cream of tartar, two household chemicals which can be purchased at a supermarket or pharmacy
- cheesecloth or a fine mesh strainer
- wool, cotton, linen or other natural fabric pieces to test your dyes on

What to Do:

Follow these steps to make each one of your dyes:

1) Chop your dye source into small pieces.

2) Fill your container about half full of water. Add one of the chopped-up materials to the water and boil on the stove until the colour is released.

3) Filter the mixture through the cheesecloth or strainer.

4) In order to make the dye colourfast, add about 1 to 2 ml of alum for every 500 ml of liquid. If the mixture curdles, add an equal amount of cream of tartar.

5) Simmer the mixture on the stove and add your piece of fabric.

6) After 30 minutes remove the material, wring it out, and rinse under cold water to remove excess colour.

7) Hang the fabric up to dry.

Digging Deeper:

Now that you know how to extract colours from natural materials, experiment to answer the questions that might have faced early people. See if you can come up with solutions using the methods early people might have used.

- What materials produce red colours? Yellow? Blue?
- Do some natural materials work better than others? Which ones?
- Can you make new colours by combining several sources?
- How can you make brighter colours? Duller ones?
- Do all fabrics accept colour the same way? Do some hold it longer than others?
- Can the dyes be made into paints that can be brushed onto other surfaces?

TIME PROBE: Mysterious Symbols

What do the Nazca Lines Mean?

The dry desert of southern Peru is crisscrossed with hundreds of lines made centuries ago. Some go for a few metres and stop. Others continue in straight lines for kilometres. Some curve and twist in strange ways.

To the traveller on foot the lines make no sense. They often seem to have no beginning, no end and no purpose. But take the traveller in a plane over the same lines and they take on new meaning. From the air they form designs and patterns. Geometric shapes the size of several football fields stretch across the desert floor. Giant pictures of monkeys, spiders, birds and whales amuse the viewer.

Who made the figures and how it was done is no longer a mystery to archeologists. The lines are the work of an ancient coastal people, the Nazcas, who flourished between 100 B.C. and A.D. 700. They were made by lifting the top layer of dark brown stones from the desert floor to expose the lighter coloured soil underneath. Because almost no moisture falls in this region, the lines have changed little over time.

The "why" behind the lines is not so easily answered. Why would a primitive people toil to produce pictures that they themselves couldn't see completely from the ground?

Several theories have been offered. Maria Reiche, a German mathematician and astronomer, studied the Nazca lines for more than 30 years. She thoroughly explored the desert, photographing and mapping hundreds of the lines and figures. She believed that the Nazca lines were an astronomical calendar, an ancient guide to the movements of the sun, moon and stars.

Julian Knott, a British balloonist, and Jim Woodman, an American writer, believe that the Nazca may have used the lines as maps or guides for airborne travel. In fact, Knott and Woodman conducted an unusual experiment in the Peruvian desert to prove the possibility of their theory.

Using Nazca materials such as vegetable fibres and reeds to make rope, basket and finely woven fabric, the two men constructed a primitive hot air balloon. After the balloon was filled with air heated by bonfires it was released. It rose swiftly, carrying the two men over the desert floor. A sudden gust of wind brought the adventure to an unexpected end, but not before the men had proved their point. It would indeed have been possible for the Nazca to construct an air vehicle from the materials around them.

Other people have suggested that the Nazca lines have religious meaning. Perhaps they were sacred symbols enlarged upon the ground so they would be visible to distant gods. They may represent constellations or signs of an ancient zodiac. Or perhaps they were sacred pathways that linked shrines in the desert.

It is also possible that different lines served different purposes. At present no one explanation seems to totally satisfy all questions about them. The Nazca lines remain a baffling and tantalizing mystery.

A. Dozier

13. UNDERSTANDING THE PAST

The Case of THE BOY IN THE MOUNTAIN

One day in 1954 two men climbed the high peak of El Plomo, a 5 000-metre mountain near Santiago, Chile. El Plomo had been a sacred mountain of the Inca, a powerful nation of native people who once ruled much of South America. On the mountain the men hoped to find gold and silver relics, treasures of the Inca that would fetch a small fortune in the marketplace.

Near the mountain peak the searchers found three small rectangular buildings. They entered the largest one, but it seemed empty, deserted. Then as their eyes adjusted to the darkness they spotted a large flat stone on the dirt floor. Perhaps there was treasure underneath!

Grunting and wheezing, the men pried the heavy slab loose and slid it along the floor. Freezing air poured from a metre-square cavity. In the blackness below they saw splatters of colour — red, yellow, white. They chattered excitedly, then suddenly grew quiet. At the bottom of the shallow pit they could see something else — the body of a small boy.

Photo by Loren MacIntyre

The youngster was about eight or nine years old. He sat huddled, his knees drawn up tightly to his chest. His arms were wrapped around his legs, his left hand clutching his right. His head leaned gently on his knees.

The boy was dressed in an unusual fashion. A band of wool encircled his head, holding a crest of black and white condor feathers in place. His body was covered in a black tunic decorated with red woollen fringes. He wore leather fur-trimmed moccasins, a small silver bracelet, and a necklace-like ornament. His face had been painted red with yellow stripes and his long hair had been carefully arranged in fine braids.

At the boy's feet lay two small golden figures, one of a llama, the other of a god in a feather headdress. Several bags were found on his body and on the dirt floor around him. Two were packed with cocao leaves. Others held samples of human hair, nail cuttings, baby teeth and pieces of red wool.

The boy looked peacefully asleep, his body perfectly preserved. But it was obvious from his clothing and the objects in the tomb that he had been frozen there for many years.

For a while the two men hovered over the body talking in whispers. It was clear to them that this was an important find, one that could fetch a handsome sum. But who would be interested in the body? What should they do with it? Finally they decided to move the body down the mountain, store it somewhere in town, then search for an interested buyer.

Carefully the men bundled up the small boy and the objects that surrounded him. A few days later they approached officials at the National Museum of Natural History in Santiago. They brought along a few of the artifacts from the tomb and told of their strange find on El Plomo. Eventually the officials purchased the body for the museum.

Freezing temperatures on the mountain peak had kept the boy's body in excellent condition. To preserve it now, the museum staff stored it in a refrigerated case. Then a team of experts went to work to unravel the mystery of the boy in the mountain. Just who was this child? And how did he come to be buried in his lonely tomb?

The youngster's clothing and possessions provided the first clues. The black woollen tunic, condor feather headdress and silver ornaments suggested that the boy was an Inca, possibly of the Altiplano tribe which had once inhabited the high mountain regions. Quite likely he was the son of a nobleman or a wealthy member of the tribe.

Tissue samples, fingerprint impressions and X-rays supplied more information. They showed that the boy had lived 500 years ago and that he had been alive when he entered the tomb. After the slab of rock had been moved into place, the sub-zero temperatures on the mountain had quickly taken their toll. The boy had probably fallen into a deep sleep before freezing to death. Then he remained undisturbed in the darkness until the two treasure seekers arrived on the mountain.

But why had the boy been buried in such a way? It was obvious that he had not been thoughtlessly dumped in the pit. A ritual had been followed. His face had been painted red, a colour the Incas were known to use in special ceremonies. His hair had been painstakingly combed and arranged. Several of the pouches he carried had been filled with carefully chosen souvenirs of his life. The other pouches had been stuffed with coca leaves, a source of cocaine that could deaden hunger and cold when chewed.

Oddly enough, although the boy's moccasins were almost new, his feet were covered with heavy calluses. In the weeks before his death he must have walked a great distance. The new moccasins had been put on his feet only at the end of his journey.

More clues came from El Plomo itself. Two sets of buildings were found on the mountain when it was investigated. The first, a temple, was located a little over 200 metres from the peak. The second, the three rectangular buildings with the boy's tomb, was closer to the top. All the buildings pointed in the same direction.

With the information provided by the body, the artifacts and the site itself, and with information already known about the Incas, the story of the boy's final days began to unfold.

●●●

The Inca priests watched the sky with concern. Each day was becoming a little shorter, each night a little longer. With each passing the sun swept lower across the sky.

The sun god must be displeased, the priests realized. It was time to go to the "hiracca", the holy place on top of the mountain. There, high above the earth, an offering must be made. If the sun god was pleased with the tribute, this journey into darkness would surely end.

But the offering had to be special. It had to be the most perfect gift the people could give. What better honour than to give the sun the healthiest and most beautiful of their own — a child.

From their ranks a young boy was chosen. He was eight years old, in good health, the son of an important member of the tribe. Surely such an offering would please the god.

Once all was ready, the priests, the elders and the young boy began their journey. They walked for hundreds of kilometres across plains and valleys to the sacred mountain. They climbed its steep surface to reach the temple near its summit.

In the temple the boy was carefully dressed and groomed. Red and yellow, the colours of the sun, were used against black, the colour of darkness. Pouches containing nail clippings, hair and teeth were prepared so that the boy would not have to search for them in the afterworld. His hair was held in place with a condor headdress, the symbol of his tribe. New moccasins were put on his callused feet.

The priests did what they could to prepare the boy for his time in the tomb. He was shown how to use coca leaves to ward off hunger and cold. Then he was given chica beer, a potion that would make him sleepy as he waited for the freezing mountain temperatures to release his spirit to the warmth of the sun god.

Finally, with all ready, a procession wound its way up the final metres to the rectangular building on the snowy summit of El Plomo. The boy was placed in the hole in the floor inside. The drug had already begun to take hold. His body and mind begged for sleep. In this foggy state he barely heard the rock slab slide over the opening.

●●●

Five hundred years have passed. Today the boy from the mountain sleeps in death inside a refrigerated showcase in a museum in Santiago. His head still rests on his knees. His arms are still wrapped around his legs, his left hand clutching his right. He still looks at peace, forever frozen in time.

DETECTIVE FILE #13
NOTES: The Archeologist's Report

Throughout a dig, hypotheses are developed, tested, refined and redefined. Some are strengthened and verified with further study. Others are discarded in favour of new ones.

After the excavation is complete, after artifacts, bones and other evidence from the past have been catalogued, analyzed and interpreted, a final report must be prepared. Through written information, charts and illustrations, the archeologist presents the evidence and all conclusions drawn from it.

A complete site report is necessary to make the information gathered by an archeologist useful. Only when other investigators have an opportunity to examine the evidence and consider it does the procedure of making and testing hypotheses and inferences become complete.

Photographs and drawings are used throughout a report. Photographs provide a record of the site, its surrounding terrain, the placement of objects as they are unearthed, and the kinds of artifacts located at the site.

Drawings are often used when simplicity and clarity are needed. Through sketches, features on artifacts can be highlighted as appropriate. Buildings or artifacts can be pictured in a reconstructed state. People can even be shown living as they once lived. In this way drawings are used to bring an archeologist's interpretations of the past to life.

The first part of a site report is an introduction to the dig. The archeologist explains the importance of the site, how it was located, and the goals of the dig. The exact location and characteristics of the site are made clear. Names of dig staff, technicians and assisting scientists are mentioned.

Another section of the report covers the methods that were used during the dig. Here the archeologist explains the techniques used to survey and excavate the site, to sort and identify the artifacts, and to analyze and interpret the results.

In a third section the evidence itself is presented. Artifacts are listed and described. Maps showing finds and features are included. Measurements and statistics are tabulated. Reports from scientists and technicians on the team are reviewed. This straightforward presentation of the evidence allows other archeologists to consider it on its own merit.

In a fourth part of the report the findings are interpreted. The archeologist summarizes the data, compares it to previous studies, draws inferences, and tries to give an overall picture of the site and its place in history. This section reflects the archeologist's own interpretations of the excavation.

In a concluding section the archeologist evaluates the dig, assessing its success and importance. Questions and problems that require further study are raised, and suggestions for future digs are posed. This section fits the site into the ongoing investigation of the past that all detectives of time are concerned with.

DETECTIVE CHALLENGE: Deciphering Evidence

Imagine that it is the year 3050. Archeologist Dr. Carol Bailey has unearthed the remains of a twentieth century home. Dr. Bailey has carefully measured, catalogued, described and analyzed each artifact taken from the site.

Here are some of her records. Can you figure out what three twentieth century items she has found?

Item 1:
   Shape: rectangular, with wedge-shaped ends
   Size: about 6 cm by 2 cm by 1 cm
   Colour: pink
   Material: rubber

Distinguishing features: worn away in irregular fashion at one end

Location: in a plastic box with numerous tubular plastic artifacts and small quantities of wood, carbon and ink

Item 2:

Shape: disk-like

Size: about two cm thick, 10 cm in diameter

Colour: black

Material: rubber

Distinguishing features: some shallow scratches on the surface

Location: in a large fabric receptacle with other fabric and plastic artifacts; among them are two identical leather artifacts with thin metal blades attached vertically to a flat surface.

Item 3:

Shape: flat, square

Size: about 14 cm by 14 cm by 1 mm

Colour: black, with white section in one corner

Material: plastic; white section is remnant of paper overlaying the plastic

Distinguishing features: circular hole in the centre; notch on one edge; several symbols visible on paper surface

Location: in a plastic box with other similar items, each of which bears different symbols; all items have symbols B and M in common

ANSWERS

Item 1 — eraser

Item 2 — hockey puck

Item 3 — computer diskette

Digging Deeper:

Try to write up similar descriptions of other objects and challenge your friends to identify them. Remember to include clear descriptions using terms that an archeologist unfamiliar with the culture would use. Provide only the kind of evidence that would survive the passage of a thousand years. See how much or how little evidence is necessary to make an object recognizable.

DETECTIVE CHALLENGE:
Making a Personal Time Capsule

Sometimes a time capsule is used to mark a special occasion. Specially selected items are locked away in a container. Then in ten, twenty or perhaps a hundred years, the container is supposed to be opened and its contents examined. Each item will help people of that future time to understand the habits, customs and lives of people in the past.

A personal time capsule is a fun way to tell your own story. By locking away specially chosen mementos you capture the present. In the future when you open your time capsule, you will have clues to your past, a record of your life as it once was.

What things would make good clues about the life you are living now? Photographs? Trophies and ribbons? Notebooks or tests from school? Autographs of friends? A list of your likes and dislikes? How about an audio or video recording of yourself and your family? Or a list of predictions for yourself?

Spend some time carefully considering what you will include in your time capsule. Find a suitable container. A sturdy cardboard box with a lid will do. Because the box is not airtight it will be able to "breathe." That means that air and moisture particles will be able to move in it, and mould and decay will not be able to start.

Line the box with high quality paper. Then wrap each item in paper too. This will prevent acid in the cardboard from damaging the articles, or one object from damaging another. Label each item with pencil.

Close the box and place it in a safe, dry place away from heat and dampness.

When will you open it? In five years? In ten?

What will its hidden treasures tell you about your past?

TIME PROBE: Mysterious Artifact

The Crystal Skull of Doom

In the living room of Anna Mitchell-Hedges of Kitchener, Ontario a life-size crystal skull rests in a felt-lined case. In the light the skull's highly polished surface glimmers and shines. Some say its empty eye sockets glow eerily as if powered by some hidden force. Some say they have seen the future in them.

The skull has been nicknamed the Crystal Skull of Doom. Over sixty years ago Mitchell-Hedges discovered it beneath an altar in the vine-choked ruins of a Mayan temple. Since then it has attracted the attention of scientists, journalists, faith-healers and the just plain curious.

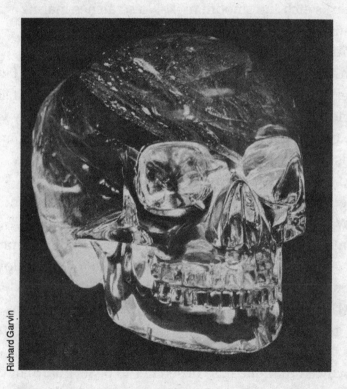

Richard Garvin

Some believe the skull is a genuine artifact once used by Mayan priests in mystical ceremonies. Others believe it is a carefully crafted forgery, the product of modern hands. Still others maintain that the skull was made by an unknown early civilization, or that it was made not by humans but by aliens instead.

The skull is steeped in mystery. So far, many of the questions that baffle scientists remain unanswered.

How old is the skull? Because there is no satisfactory technique for dating crystal, scientists have not been able to pinpoint a date. Those who believe it to be genuine maintain that the skull could be 12 000 years old. Those who believe it is a forgery say that it was made much later, perhaps in the 1800s.

How was the skull carved and shaped? It is transparent, made of hard quartz crystal. If ancient Maya made the skull by patiently grinding and rubbing pure rock crystal, scientists estimate it would have taken several lifetimes to achieve the task. Yet no evidence suggests that modern instruments were used. No tool marks etch the smooth rock. No scratches mar its polished surface.

How did the skull come into Anna Mitchell-Hedges' possession? A proper report was never published, so few facts of its discovery are known. Mitchell-Hedges says simply that she found the top half of the skull on her seventeenth birthday while she was excavating an ancient Mayan city with her father, an archeologist. Three months later its detachable jaw was discovered a short distance away.

The vagueness of the story has stirred doubts in the minds of skeptics. Was the skull really discovered in the Mayan city? Or was it planted beneath the altar, perhaps as a birthday surprise for Anna? And why did it take three months to locate the lower half of the skull when it was so close by?

Anna Mitchell-Hedges shrugs off the puzzling questions. She refuses to give the skull to a museum. In her mind the Crystal Skull is an authentic Mayan artifact with a vibrant life of its own. She is convinced that fate has chosen her to be its guardian. So the skull rests in its felt-lined case in her home, a thing of beauty, an object of constant mystery.

14. WORKING AS A TEAM

The Case of THE TITANIC: LOST AND REDISCOVERED

Of all sunken ships the *Titanic* is the most famous.

The *Titanic*, built in 1911, was billed as "the wondership," "the unsinkable ship" and "the last word in luxury." Almost as long as four city blocks and as tall as an eleven-storey building, she was the world's largest passenger ship. Everything about her was oversized — the nine decks stacked one on top of the other, the funnels as wide as highways, the propellers the size of windmills.

The ship was designed for comfort as well. She sported sumptuous dining rooms, elegant dance halls, squash courts, a gymnasium, and one of the first swimming pools on an ocean liner. The *Titanic's* builders boasted about her safety. She had been constructed with 16 watertight compartments in her hull. If danger threatened, the compartments could be sealed so that water would not spill from one into the next.

On Wednesday, April 10, 1912, the *Titanic* left Southampton, England on her maiden voyage. Carrying 2227 passengers and crew, she headed across the Atlantic towards New York.

By Sunday, April 14, the ship was more than halfway to her destination. Her radio crackled with warnings from neighbouring ships: "Proceed cautiously. Icebergs ahead."

That night the ocean was calm, the air bitterly cold. Just before midnight a lookout spotted a huge ghostly shape directly ahead of the ship. He sounded the alarm bell three times and telephoned the chief officer in the ship's bridge.

"Iceberg ahead," he reported.

Immediately orders were issued — reverse the engines, change course, close the doors to the watertight compartments. Because of her size, however, the speed and direction of the 45 000 tonne vessel could not be changed quickly. The Titanic continued to plow ahead, avoiding a head-on collision but scraping her starboard side against the iceberg. Below the waterline the hull started to take on water.

The *Titanic* had been designed to remain afloat even if the first four compartments in the bow flooded. But the damage was even greater than that. Water gushed into the first tank, three of the forward holds and one of the boiler rooms. When these five compartments were filled, other compartments began to flood as well. It was more than the ship's design could handle.

As the forward sections flooded, the bow of the *Titanic* began to dip noticeably. Calls for help were broadcast over the ship's radio and distress rockets were fired into the air. Passengers and crew assembled on the decks. While a band played lively music to keep up everyone's spirits, lifeboats were loaded with women and children and set afloat.

By 2:05 A.M., almost two hours after the collision, all the lifeboats had been set adrift. Over 1500 people still remained on board. Because of their confidence in the Titanic's safety, her buiders had not provided enough lifeboats for more than half of the passengers.

An eerie calm settled over the ship. As more of the bow sank below the surface the stern began to rise out of the water. People quietly huddled together, gradually moving to higher areas as water edged up the decks.

At approximately 2:20 A.M.. a shudder ran through the ship. The *Titanic* lurched suddenly, her bow plunging downward, her stern rising almost upright. People clutched ropes and railings; many fell or jumped overboard. For a few minutes more the ship remained visible. Then slowly she slipped below the surface and disappeared into the icy Atlantic.

Alerted by the *Titanic's* distress calls, neighbouring ships steamed to her aid. At 4:00 A.M. the first ship arrived to begin plucking 705 survivors from lifeboats. The remaining 1522 passengers and crew drowned or froze to death in the frigid water.

After the tragedy many people dreamed of finding the luxury liner. Overwhelming obstacles stood in their way. Although the *Titanic's* last radioed position had been 640 kilometres southeast of Newfoundland, her exact location was unknown. The search area covered over 250 square kilometres of ocean averaging three to five kilometres in depth. Gullies, crevices and deep canyons along the bottom provided numerous hiding places for the wreck. Finding any ship, even one as large as the *Titanic*, in an area so wide, so deep and so rugged was akin to finding a needle in a haystack.

Ocean conditions would hamper search efforts too. Rocked by storms, crossed by strong currents, plugged with ice much of the year, the unpredictable Atlantic would make any search difficult and hazardous.

But the biggest problem was ocean depth. The *Titanic* lay at the bottom of four kilometres of water. At this depth sunlight cannot penetrate the water, temperatures hover near the freezing point, and the weight of the water exerts tremendously crushing pressures.

Even if by some stroke of good fortune the ship could be located, how would she be reached? With ordinary equipment exploration at such depths was impossible. A well-equipped scuba diver might safely descend to 100 metres; a naval submarine to perhaps 600 metres. But four kilometres?

For decades the Titanic remained a lost and unreachable target. But by the 1980s new equipment and techniques had changed the face of undersea exploration. Stronger, more resilient alloys enabled submarines to withstand the tremendous pressures of deep dives. Improved tracking systems made underwater scanning more accurate. Video equipment and remote-controlled devices allowed searchers to see below the water without even entering it.

Robert D. Ballard, an American marine geologist, had helped to pioneer the new technology. Its success convinced him that at last the *Titanic* was within reach. For years he interviewed experts, read historical records, poured over maps and charts, and talked enthusiastically about leading a search for the wreck.

In 1985 Ballard persuaded the Woods Hole Oceanographic Institute to participate in a joint French-American expedition to locate the *Titanic*. The French had developed an efficient sonar instrument. Shaped like a torpedo, towed by cable just above the ocean floor, the device sent electronic sound pulses into the water. Tracking the reflected sound waves produced a type of shadow picture that revealed shapes and contours along the bottom.

Ballard's own research involved the use of remote-controlled camera systems to scan and film the ocean bottom. This would provide a degree of detail impossible with only sonar. Combining the French equipment with Ballard's visual tracking system offered promising results.

The scientific team decided on a two-phase search plan. In the first phase the sonar "torpedo" on the French ship *Le Suroit* would sweep the ocean bottom, identifying possible targets for closer examination. In the second phase the visual equipment aboard the American ship *Knorr* would be used to inspect and photograph the target sites. But the search would be limited to a few short weeks. Finding the *Titanic* in that brief period would require plenty of good fortune as well as skill.

The first part of the search proved frustrating and fruitless. Suspended by a cable kilometres long, the sonar torpedo dangled just above the ocean floor, precariously bobbing and bouncing as *Le Suroit* was tossed by ocean storms and strong currents. Despite numerous passes over a large part of the search area, no trace of the *Titanic* was found.

After several weeks the expedition moved onto the *Knorr*. As leader of this phase of the search, Ballard decided on a new approach. Instead of trying to find the *Titanic* itself, barely a speck on the ocean floor, his team would concentrate on searching for the debris that must have been scattered as the ship went down. Searching for this wider target, Ballard reasoned, would improve his chance of finding evidence of the *Titanic*. And the visual method his team used to check the ocean floor was well adapted to spotting small objects.

Le Suroit had already covered most of the search area. Ballard decided to start his visual scan in the unsearched section. If the Titanic could not be found there, then the searched area would be rechecked in case the sonar had somehow missed the ship.

The *Knorr* was equipped with *Argo*, a steel sled-like device mounted with video cameras. *Argo* was lowered by cable into the water and towed just above the bottom, its headlights piercing the murky blackness. Images from its video cameras were relayed to monitors on board the research vessel.

Keeping *Argo* suspended at just the right depth was difficult. Too far away and the images were hazy; too close and *Argo* threatened to collide into hills and rises.

For days *Argo* transmitted images of the muddy bottom to monitors on board the *Knorr*. The task of watching the images became tedious and boring; the crew grew restless. Hope of finding the *Titanic* seemed more remote with each pass of *Argo*.

The night of August 31 seemed no more eventful than usual. *Argo* continued to relay pictures of the monotonous bottom. Then shortly after midnight a different shape appeared on the screen — something metallic, something man-made.

"Wreckage," one of the crew whispered.

"Bingo!" another shouted.

Shrieks and cries filled the control room. People clustered around the monitors, talking in excited voices as more and more chunks of debris appeared.

Argo found many pieces of wreckage scattered around the ocean floor — twisted bulkheads, mangled steel plates, a badly bent crane from the ship's deck. This was the trail of debris and wreckage left by the *Titanic* as she sank through the water and smashed into the muddy ocean bottom 73 years earlier.

A map of the debris field was made by plotting the position of each piece of wreckage. From it, the probable position of the ship itself was targeted. Finally *Argo* made a sweep of the pinpointed site. In the glare of the headlights a wall of steel rose from the ocean floor. At last, the *Titanic*.

Argo passed over the deck of the ship, relaying a steady stream of images to the crew. To their surprise the ship was upright but not intact. The stern was missing.

With only hours left in the expedition there was no time for a complete search. Photographs were taken of the bow and the debris field, then the *Knorr* had to head back to port.

The following year Ballard and his team returned to the site to continue their research. Using *Alvin*, a tiny deep-water submarine Ballard had helped to develop, they descended to the wreck. The stern section lay 600 metres from the bow. With the help of a remote-controlled robot called *Jason Junior*, Ballard explored both sections inside and out, taking scores of pictures. Many features of the luxurious liner were still identifiable.

Woods Hole Oceanographic Institute

A set of stairs from the once luxurious *Titanic*

Thousands of objects littered the ocean floor between the bow and the stern. Like toys dumped across a playroom floor, bathtubs, sinks, heaters, boilers, ladders and other parts of the ship poked through the thick ooze. Among these larger items lay smaller things, personal objects that had once belonged to the passengers and crew of the *Titanic*.

On one sweep of the debris field Ballard and his crew saw a pair of matching shoes lying side by side on the ocean floor. Nearby they found another pair, then a third. Clearly the shoes hadn't landed together by accident. At one time victims must have been wearing them. Although the bodies had long since decayed and disappeared, the shoes remained as silent witnesses to their owners' fate.

What actually happened on that tragic April night in 1912? Thousands of photographs and hours of videotape of the wreckage have made the story of the *Titanic's* last hours clearer.

From the time of the sinking it was assumed that a jagged edge of ice had ripped into the bow of the ship and left puncture holes in enough of the hull to flood the five forward sections. But Ballard's examination suggested that when the iceberg glanced across the ship, some of the hull's steel plates popped apart at the seams. Water gushed into the ship through the resulting cracks, not through holes.

It was also long believed that the *Titanic* might have sunk in one piece. But the expedition proved a different story. As the forward sections filled, the bow dipped lower, gradually hoisting the stern into the air. As a result, tremendous pressure was exerted on the steel hull, which finally buckled and snapped into two pieces.

The bow started its downward plunge immediately. But the stern section swung around and remained upright for a short time before disappearing below the surface. The bow hit the bottom first. A few minutes later the stern smashed into the mud facing in the other direction. For hours afterward debris from the ship drifted down and settled around the wreck.

Ballard and his team made many descents to the *Titanic*. On one of these they left a memorial plaque on the stern of the ship, a tribute to all those who died in the tragedy. But they didn't disturb the vessel itself. In this case, excavating the site would not have revealed any more than Ballard's visual examination did.

After the final dive the crew climbed the four kilometres to the surface leaving the *Titanic*, the greatest of all shipwrecks, exactly as it had been found — untouched at the bottom of the ocean.

DETECTIVE FILE #14
NOTES: The Modern Archeological Team

In the early days of archeology a small team of people might locate, survey and excavate a site. Later, in the lab, the same people might clean and catalogue the artifacts and interpret the evidence.

Today the methods and procedures of archeology are much more refined and much more complex. Archeologists do not work alone. They rely on the expertise and talents of volunteers, technicians and specialists. They also work in partnership with other time-detective scientists to develop a complete picture of the events that have occurred over time. Modern archeology is very much a team effort, both in the field and in the lab.

You have already met some of the members of an archeological team through the stories and notes presented in this book. But there are others as well. Here is a list of some of the people who help archeologists unravel the mysteries of time.

OTHER SCIENTISTS:

The Botanist gathers evidence from seeds, pollen, decayed plant materials and fossils to provide information about the plants that once grew in the region.

The Geologist studies rocks, minerals and formations in order to understand the events that shaped the land, and provides the archeologist with information about the materials and resources that were available to early people.

The Paleontologist studies and analyzes fossils in order to learn about prehistoric plants and animals that once occupied the site.

The Pedologist examines and analyzes the soil at the site to learn about the soil layers and their chemical composition.

The Physical Anthropologist measures and analyzes human remains to help the archeologist learn about the appearance, health, origins and habits of early people.

The Paleoanthropologist studies the fossil remains of our early ancestors, members of the human family known as hominids.

The Zoologist provides information about the animals that once occupied the area by examining animal skeletons, mummified remains and imprints in rock and stone.

OTHER EXPERTS:

The Artist makes sketches of artifacts and other features, using information from the dig to recreate the site through drawings.

The Ceramist identifies and restores pottery, earthenware, tile and porcelain.

The Draftsman records the exact position of all fossils and artifacts as they are excavated.

The Epigraphist studies and decodes inscriptions and writings.

The Photographer takes pictures of artifacts and fossils as they are uncovered, being careful to show their location and size in proper perspective, and also photographs artifacts after they have been prepared in the lab.

The Registrar classifies, catalogues, labels and stores artifacts.

The Surveyor surveys the site and draws precise maps of the site area before the dig.

DETECTIVE CHALLENGE: Getting Field Experience

Do you want to learn more about the ways of an archeological team? Do you want practical experience in the field? Here are three ways to get involved.

I. Join an Archeological Organization or Club

Many cities have archeological clubs. Some are geared especially toward young people. When you join such a club you meet with others who share your interest in archeology. Together you do activities, go on tours, talk to archeologists and perhaps even participate in an actual dig. Contact your local museum for information, or check the yellow pages of your phone book under Associations or Organizations for the names of archeological societies near you.

II. Volunteer at a Dig Site

There are many archeological digs across the country. Sometimes archeologists enlist the help of volunteers at these sites. Working side-by-side with skilled professionals can give you valuable training in the ways of archeology.

Contact a museum or archeological society or club for information about ongoing digs. Ask if there is some way that you can volunteer at a dig site.

III. Conduct a Simulated Dig (an activity for 2 or more people)

If you can not participate in an actual archeological dig, you can use a simulated dig to try your hand at excavation and interpretation. Simulated means artificial instead of real. A simulated dig involves two teams, one to bury evidence in the soil, the other to unearth and interpret it. Both teams gain experience in the techniques of archeology learned in this book.

Start by rounding up the equipment needed by each group.

Materials:
Team 1
- objects to bury: broken pottery or china,
  coins, nails, bits of cloth, wood or leather, bones, etc.
- four wooden stakes or long metal spikes
- string
- a hammer
- graph or grid paper
- pencil
- digging tools: small spade and trowel
- ruler

Team 2
- graph or grid paper
- pencil
- ruler
- digging tools: trowel, paintbrush, toothbrush

What to Do:
Team 1: Hiding the Evidence
Buried artifacts tell a story of the past. In this exercise you want to tell a story with the objects you bury. You want to leave clues for the excavating team so that they can figure out your story.

1) Determine what story you want to tell. Do you want the excavating team to think that the objects were deposited over a long period of time or buried in a single day? That the objects belonged to a single person or to a group of people? That they were lost accidentally or purposely hidden? That the objects are separate and unrelated or that they belong together like pieces of a puzzle?

You can tell your story by carefully choosing your objects and planning their burial. The kinds of things you bury, their depth underground, their position compared to other objects — these are clues that the excavating team will use to unravel your story.

For instance, if you bury several pieces of similar-looking pottery side by side, the excavating team may infer that the pieces were once part of something larger and were likely buried at the same time. Perhaps they will be able to reconstruct the object. If you include some dated objects — a coin and a section of newspaper, for example — at different levels, the excavating team may be able to track down the order of burial and infer a different story.

2) Once you have decided on the clues you will hide, select a site outdoors. Look for a place that has soft soil or sand and is fairly level or flat.

3) Mark off a square about 50 cm by 50 cm (larger if you want a greater challenge). Hammer in stakes or spikes at each corner of the square. Tie string from corner to corner to fence in the square.

4) Using the spade, dig out the soil to a depth of 15 cm and set it aside.

5) Use the grid paper to make a top plan of the square as you refill it and bury your objects. This will be a record of the evidence you have hidden. Decide on the scale you wish to use, then use the ruler to outline the square on the paper. When you bury an object in the square, measure its distance from each string, then draw it in position on the grid paper. To show its depth measure the object's distance below ground level and record this measurement beside the picture.

6) Once you have buried all of the objects, smooth out the top layer of soil to make the site look as undisturbed as possible. Leave the site so that Team 2 can excavate the square.

Team 2: Unearthing the Evidence

As the excavating team, your goal is to unearth the objects in the square, record their position on a top plan, and interpret the evidence so as to unravel a story from the past.

1) First make a top plan of the square. Measure the square, decide on your scale, and outline the square on grid paper. As you uncover each object measure its distance from the strings and draw it on the top plan. Measure its depth below the surface too, and record that beside your drawing of the object.

2) Use the trowel to scrape away thin layers of soil. Work slowly and carefully. If you hurry you may miss a small object or knock it out of position.

3) When you encounter an object dust if off with the paint brush. Use the toothbrush to remove any stubborn clumps of dirt. Before removing the object from the square, plot it on the top plan.

4) Once you have uncovered all the items study the objects and the top plan carefully. Ask yourself questions. Can you establish times or dates? Do the objects relate or connect in some way? Do they appear to have been left by one person or several? What is the story behind the evidence?

Once the excavating team has interpreted the evidence, the two teams should meet to share results. Compare top plans. How alike are they? Are there any objects that were missed, incorrectly measured or improperly plotted on the grid?

Compare stories. How alike are they? Was the message the excavating team got the one the burying team wanted to leave? If not, why?

How could the archeological skills of each team be improved?

TIME PROBE: Puzzling Structures

Explaining Stonehenge and the Great Pyramid

Long before the time of Christ early man built remarkable structures of stone. Using only primitive tools, immense stone slabs were cut, carved and hoisted into carefully designed shapes. Because stone survives the passage of time better than most materials, many of these structures can be seen even today. Unfortunately the original plans and purposes of their ancient builders have not endured as well. Are these massive structures monuments, tombs, or were they built for other reasons?

Here are two timeless structures. Both have been studied by many teams working over the years. A lot has been learned about them, but many questions remain. The structures continue to puzzle and intrigue us thousands of years after they were first constructed.

Stonehenge

One of the most impressive and mysterious of ancient structures is Stonehenge in England. This great stone circle stands alone on a flat plain. Immense stone pillars support gracefully curved stone cross slabs weighing up to 50 tonnes.

Photo by Paul Heersink

Stonehenge is a marvel of engineering skill. Because this monument was built before the wheel was invented, the slabs were likely moved long distances across the plain on sledges and rollers. Each stone was precisely ground and shaped. Then it was raised and fitted into place. The strength of as many as a thousand people working together might have been needed to move a single slab.

Stonehenge appears to have been built in three stages by three different sets of people. The first group constructed a circular ditch and earth enclosure around 2700 B.C. Eight hundred years later another group of people added to the structure. They carted huge boulders to the site from hills 400 kilometres away. These were set upright to form a double circle inside the earlier enclosure. Around 1500 B.C. another group of builders moved in more stone slabs. Some of these were set on end as pillars. Then other slabs were lifted and laid horizontally on top of them.

Many questions about Stonehenge remain unanswered. The positions of its stones and features suggest that it might have been used as an astronomical observatory to plot the course of the sun and moon. But was that its only purpose? What other purposes might it have served? What force was strong enough to drive thousands of people to spend hundreds of years building it? Why was it abandoned? And why did a people who were such skilled engineers, architects, mathematicians and astronomers not develop such a simple but useful tool as the wheel?

The Great Pyramid of Giza

Of the 40 pyramids that line the banks of the Nile River in Egypt, one towers above the rest. The Great Pyramid of Giza stands 150 metres high. Constructed of 2 300 000 stone blocks, this giant contains enough stone to encircle a country the size of France with a 3-metre-high fence.

Built about 4500 years ago by King Khufu of Egypt, the original pyramid was covered with slabs of gleaming white limestone. On the inside a maze of corridors and passageways led to hidden chambers. Over the centuries the pyramid has been entered and plundered many times. Its limestone surface has disappeared and its interior has been explored and mapped. Nevertheless, the Great Pyramid remains an object of mystery.

Why was the pyramid built? Most scholars believe that it was constructed to be a tomb, a tribute to its builder, King Khufu. But Khufu's mummy was never found in it. Some experts think that the pyramid might have served other purposes as well.

The walls, corridors and cavities of the pyramid are unusually precise. Its measurements are so accurate that its immense sides differ in length by only centimetres. It is aligned with true north so exactly that even today such a result would be hard to achieve. In fact, the mathematical principles illustrated in the pyramid's construction were not thought to have been discovered until thousands of years after it was built.

Many theories have been offered to explain this. Some people maintain that the pyramid was actually a gigantic calendar. Others think it was an observatory, a place where scientists could study the passage of the stars and planets. Some suggest that the pyramid was a type of calculator for computing such things as the length of the year, the speed of light and the dimensions of the earth. Still others think that it could have been an ancient library or a place for storing scientific equipment.

Whatever its purpose, the Great Pyramid remains one of the wonders of the ancient world, one of the most awesome places of mystery still waiting for future detectives of time to uncover its secrets.

AFTERWORD

A Final Note

Item by item, clue by clue, detectives of time piece together stories of the past. Each story has its own unique setting and plot, its own cast of characters. Each story is rooted in time, the invisible thread that connects the present to unknown events of long ago.

Suppose all of these stories could be collected and assembled in one large book. Suppose each page in the book represented one year. The first pages would tell about the present. The last pages would describe what we know of the beginning of the human story.

What would this book be like? What would it tell about our past?

Imagine for a moment such a book standing before you. It looks unlike any book you have ever seen before. The first thing you notice is its size. It is massive, over four million pages thick, as tall as a 60-storey building. Scientists tell us human history began over four million years ago.

The book is unusual in another way as well. It is constantly being revised and rewritten. At the end of each year a fresh page is added to the front of the book. Sometimes, as more of the past is uncovered, information is added further back. And as our understanding of the past changes, the information has to be changed too.

Now imagine opening the book. Picture yourself leafing through the pages, looking back through time.

The first few hundred pages are packed with details. The print is small and illustrations are plentiful. You recognize names and faces from the past. You recognize events and places.

But as you move further into the book the print becomes hazier, the pages more incomplete. Many pages have only a line or two on them. Some are blank. Less and less is known about these times.

A few stories stand out clearly and light the way, however. Near page 1000 you read about Vinland, the earliest known European settlement in North America. Around page 2300 you find information about Philip II of Macedon. On page 4500 you see an illustration of the Great Pyramid of Egypt.

In short order, after just five or six thousand pages, you have reached the dawn of civilization and the beginning of written language. Yet you have barely made a dent in the book. Almost four million pages remain to be explored, four million years of the past where the only evidence is fossils, bones and stones.

Quickly flip through the rest of the book, letting time fly through your fingers. Most pages are empty of information, with only a few scattered lines or paragraphs here and there. Occasionally you spot illustrations, but these only leave you confused and uncertain. The farther back you move into time, the less you recognize. By the time you are well into the book even the humans look unfamiliar. They appear shorter and hairier. Heads are smaller, jaws jut forward, foreheads slope sharply to the back. In some ways these creatures resemble apes, but their hands and feet look human and they walk upright on two legs. Do these beings really belong in a book about our past? You wonder.

Many stories in this giant book are incomplete. Others have yet to be revealed. Our human past is shadowed in mystery. It is a puzzle sealed in rock and bone, a riddle with only faint clues for guidance. To unravel the past, detectives of time must continue to gather, analyze and interpret evidence.

Will you take up the challenge? Will you be among those who someday write on these pages?

A Final Challenge

One way to start as an investigator of time might be to make a book of your own past.

Find a binder, or other booklet that allows you to insert and change pages. Add looseleaf or blank paper. You will need at least one page for each year of your life.

Number the first page of the book with your present age. The following pages will be numbered in decreasing order until you reach page 1, the first year of your life.

Now what will you put on each page? The first pages in the book will be the easiest to fill because they are the most recent. Tell the stories of your past. Jot down what you consider to have been important or memorable about each year. Add pictures, illustrations, letters from friends or relatives, samples of school work — whatever represents the things you hold important about each year of your life. Add as many pages as you need.

As you move further back in time, stories may be more difficult to recall. Details may be hazy. Be resourceful; use your detective skills. Try to get information from a variety of people, places and things.

If you wish, investigate the years before your birth too. You can number these pages with negative numbers: -1, -2. Write about the people and events that were to have a bearing on your life. How far back in time can you go? How many more stories can you include?

Update your book as time moves ahead. Each year add fresh pages to the start of the book. Write new stories as they unfold. Let your book span time. Have it link the past with the present. Let it be your bridge to the future.

And remember, anything may fall into the hands of future detectives of time. How much will your book tell them about you and your place in time?

BIBLIOGRAPHY

Andronicos, Manolis. "Regal Treasures from a Macedonian Tomb." *National Geographic*, July 1978, 154 (1), pp. 54-77.

Baldwin, Gordon C. *The Riddle of the Past: How Archaeological Detectives Solve Prehistoric Puzzles*. New York: W. W. Norton & Co., Inc., 1965.

Ballard, Robert D. "How We Found Titanic." *National Geographic*, Dec. 1985, 168 (6), pp. 696-719.

Ballard, Robert D. "Long Last Look at Titanic." *National Geographic*, Dec. 1986, 170 (6), pp. 698-727.

Ballard, Robert D. *The Discovery of the Titanic*. Toronto: Madison Publishing Inc., 1987.

Ballard, Robert D. *Exploring the Titanic*. Toronto: Madison Press Books, 1988.

Barker, Philip. *Understanding Archeological Excavation*. New York: St. Martin's Press, 1986.

Beattie, Owen & Geiger, John. *Frozen in Time*. Saskatoon: Western Producer Prairie Books, 1987.

Bertman, Stephen. *Doorways Through Time*. Los Angeles: Jeremy P. Tarcher, Inc., 1986.

Canby, Thomas Y. "The Anasazi: Riddles in the Ruins." *National Geographic*, Nov. 1982, 162 (5), pp. 554-605.

Ceram, C.W.(ed.). *Hands on the Past*. New York: Alfred A. Knopf, 1966.

Ceram, C.W. *Gods, Graves & Scholars*. New York: Alfred A. Knopf, 1985.

Colombo, John Robert. *Mysterious Canada*. Toronto: Doubleday Canada Ltd., 1988.

Corcoran, John. *The Young Field Archeologist's Guide*. London: Bell, 1966.

de Borhegyi, Suzanne. *Ships, Shoals and Amphora*. New York: Holt, Rinehart & Winston, 1961.

Donnelly, Judy. *The Titanic: Lost and Found*. New York: Random House, 1987.

Eydoux, Henri-Paul. *The Buried Past*. London: George Weidenfeld & Nicholson Ltd., 1962.

Fagan, Brian. *New Treasures of the Past*. New York: Barron's Educational Series, Inc., 1987.

Fleming, Stuart James. *Dating in Archeology: A Guide to Scientific Technique*. London: Dent, 1976.

Fourneaux, Rupert. *Ancient Mysteries*. New York: Ballantine Books, 1988.

Fradin, Dennis B. *Archeology*. Chicago: Childrens Press, 1983.

Friedman, Estelle. *Digging into Yesterday*. New York: G.P. Putman's Sons, 1958.

Gallant, Roy A. *Lost Cities*. New York: Franklin Watts, 1985.

Glubok, Shirley. *Art and Archeology*. New York: Harper and Row, 1966.

Gore, Rick. "The Dead Do Tell Tales at Vesuvius." *National Geographic*, May 1984, 165 (5), pp. 556-613.

Gore, Rick. "Extinctions." *National Geographic*, June 1989, 175 (6), pp. 662-699.

Grier, Katherine. *Discover: Mysteries of the Past and Present*. Toronto: Kids Can Press Ltd., 1989.

Hackwell, W. John. *Digging to the Past: Excavations in Ancient Lands*. New York: Charles Scribner's Sons, 1986.

Holden, Raymond. *Secrets in the Dust*. New York: Dodd, Mead & Co., 1959.

Ingstad, Helge. "Vinland Ruins Prove Vikings Found New World." *National Geographic*, Nov. 1964, 126 (5), pp. 708-734.

Jessup, Ronald. *The Wonderful World of Archeology*. New York: Doubleday and Co., Inc., 1968.

Johnstone, Paul. *The Archeology of Ships*. New York: Henry Z. Walch, Inc., 1974.

Judge, Joseph. "A Buried Town Gives Up Its Dead." *National Geographic*, Dec. 1982, 162 (6), pp. 687-692.

LaHaye, Tim F. & Morris, John D. *The Ark on Ararat*. Nashville: Thomas Nelson Inc., 1976.

Lauber, Patricia. *Tales Mummies Tell*. New York: Thomas Y. Crowell, 1985.

Linder, Elisha & Raban, Avner. *Introducing Underwater Archeology*. Minneapolis: Lerner Publications Company, 1976.

Marcus, Rebecca. *Prehistoric Cave Paintings*. New York: Franklin Watts, Inc., 1968.

Marx, Robert F. *The Underwater Dig.* New York: Henry Z. Walck, Inc., 1975.

McIntosh, Jane. *The Practical Archaeologist.* New York: Facts on File Publications, 1986.

McGee, Patricia. "Challenging History: Peaceful Women May Have Once Ruled the World." *Macleans,* Feb.12, 1990, pp. 66-67.

Millard, Anne. *Ancient Civilizations.* New York: Warwick Press, 1983.

Morrison, Vilma Ford. *Going on a Dig.* New York: Dodd, Mead & Co., 1981.

Nelson, Lisa W. *Mammoth Graveyard: A Treasure Trove of Clues to the Past.* Flagstaff, Arizona: Northern Arizona University, 1988.

Newlands, David L. and Claus Breede. *An Introduction to Canadian Archaeology.* Toronto: McGraw-Hill Ryerson Ltd., 1976

Porell, Bruce. *Digging the Past: Archaeology in Your Own Backyard.* Massachusetts: Addison-Wesley, 1979.

Rackl, Hanns-Wolf. *Diving into the Past: Archaeology Underwater.* New York: Charles Scribner's Sons, 1968.

Raintree Publishers. *Archeology.* Milwaukee: Raintree Publishers, 1988.

Reader's Digest. *The World's Last Mysteries.* New York: The Reader's Digest Association, Inc., 1978.

Reader's Digest. *Vanished Civilizations.* Sydney: Reader's Digest Services, 1983.

Schiller, Ronald. *Distant Secrets: Unravelling the Mysteries of Our Ancient Past.* New York: Carol Publishing Groups, 1989.

Seff, Philip & Seff, Nancy R. *Our Fascinating Earth.* Chicago: Contemporary Books, Inc., 1990.

Stuart, Gene S. *Secrets from the Past.* National Geographic Society, 1979.

Suggs, Robert C. *Modern Discoveries in Archeology.* New York: Anchor Press, 1988.

Sullivan, George. *Discover Archaeology: An Introduction to the Tools and Techniques of Archaeological Fieldwork.* Garden City, N.Y.: Doubleday & Co., Inc., 1980.

Thorndike, Joseph J. Jr.(ed.) *Discovery of Lost Worlds.* New York: American Heritage Publishing Co. Inc., 1979.

Trease, Geoffrey. *Hidden Treasure.* London: Hamish Hamilton Children's Books, 1989.

Ventura, Piero & Gian Paolo Ceserani. *In Search of Ancient Crete.* Morristown, N.J., Silver Burdett Co., 1985.

Ventura, Piero & Gian Paolo Ceserani. *In Search of Pompeii.* Morristown, N.J., Silver Burdett Co., 1985.

Ward, Anne. *Adventures in Archeology.* New York: Larousse & Co., Ltd., 1977.

Watson, Don. *Cliff Dwellings of the Mesa Verde.* Colorado: Mesa Verde Museum Association.

Wheeler, Margaret. *History Was Buried.* New York: Galahad Books, 1967.

Wilson, Ian. *Undiscovered: The Fascinating World of Undiscovered Places, Graves, Wrecks and Treasure.* Great Britain: Michael O'Mara Books Ltd., 1987.

Credits and Acknowledgements

Figures 3 and 4 on page 29 reproduced from *Understanding Archaeological Excavation* by Philip Barker, courtesy of the publisher, B T Batsford Ltd.

Photo page 156 courtesy of the Royal Ontario Museum, Toronto, Canada.

Photo page 164 courtesy Larry Verstraete.

Thanks to Chris McGowan, David Newlands and Peta Daniels for the site work photos throughout.

Every effort has been made to identify and credit appropriately the source of all photographs reproduced in this book. Any further information will be appreciated and acknowledged in subsequent editions.

About the Author

Larry Verstraete's first book, *The Serendipity Effect*, began as a class assignment in a course on children's literature. A teacher by profession, Larry claims that he always had a secret ambition to become a published writer. Well, the secret's out — and we're all a little wiser for it!

Larry lives in Winnipeg, Manitoba, with his wife and two children. In his spare time he works on his hobbies — carpentry and stained glass — and, of course, on his next science book.